# Praise for this book

*"I enjoyed reading the book. It is written in a friendly and user focussed manner, with the best interests of students at its core.*

*What did I like about the book?*

✓ *User friendly style*

✓ *Well thought out resource to help in the development of transferable skills relevant to study and work*

✓ *Excellent range of practical examples to aid the development of students as they progress through their learning journey*

✓ *Good prompts and direction given for those needing additional guidance, support or information beyond this resource."*

*Professor Craig Mahoney, Chief Executive, Higher Education Academy*

*"As a comprehensive yet highly accessible resource Angela's publication is likely to be of great value for staff and students alike. Helping students to 'make the most' of their experience, academically and personally, and how to present this effectively, is essential. This publication, grounded in direct experience of working with students, provides a wonderfully practical route to effectively address key challenges."*
*Rob Ward, Director, The Centre for Recording Achievement*

*"I think the book provides a comprehensive, user-friendly toolkit for students that could help ensure they maximise their investment in their education and employability."* Senior careers officer

*"I will certainly be encouraging my students to use this book and I will be definitely be using some of the exercises in my training sessions."*
*Donna Berwick, Skills and Recognition Office, University of Salford*

3

PRAISE FOR THIS BOOK

*"I really like the book and as a guide to making the most of a higher education course I think it is excellent. It is student friendly, easy to work through and the exercises are great."*
*Teaching Fellow for Employability*

*"I'm not an academic but work extensively on my college's learning and teaching strategy and all associated issues so your book was very useful to cut through all the hyperbole etc surrounding PDP.*
*Your book demystifies PDP with a refreshing, straightforward and easy to read style. It is an invaluable aid to studying and learning."*
*Academic Affairs Officer*

*"With study skills and personal development planning underpinning the learning of undergraduate students, this text will be an invaluable introduction to students negotiating the pathways of academia. This book offers an appropriate rationale for the place of PDP on University courses, while allowing the reader opportunities to complete logical exercises designed to develop their academic skills. The sections on critical reading and writing will be of benefit to students wishing to extend their thinking and developing their critical analysis. There are numerous practical ideas for staff delivering PDP as part of their teaching."* Senior Lecturer

*"The way you do one thing, is usually the way you do everything. If you engage fully with this book and not only read it but actually do all the exercises, it will transform your life.*
*This book is an absolute must for any student who is seriously intent on achieving high grades and then continuing on to be highly successful in life. This is a book for life - don't just read it, use it. Take action."* Life coach

*"The book covers all of the key elements required by students in helping them to develop the essential key skills to help them through their course. It also provides essential information and advice on how students can enhance their employability and make themselves more attractive to employers. The way the book is organised into key, easy to follow chapters, providing valuable information and student tasks and activities means that it can form a personal development portfolio in itself if followed and is beneficial to both staff and students alike ensuring coverage of the essential elements."* Senior lecturer

*"Congratulations on an excellent publication. It reads well and I think it is student-friendly."*

*"I especially loved the chapter on goal setting. It is sometimes so good to have a focus to reach your goals and aspirations. With your help and guidance everything is possible."*

# What students like about this book:

*"This book has been a great read with its simple straight to the point and well organised content; helping me to succeed and get the most out of what I want to achieve for the future. It has also helped me, during my studies at university, with scientific lab reports, dissertations and lecture note taking. I am now able to structure and write my work to a high standard.*
*This book has been excellent help for my future career, helping me to design a well formatted CV, personal statement and more importantly teaching me a helpful and clear approach to interview technique, essential for graduates."*
*First Year Undergraduate, Liverpool University*

*"The book has a fantastic skills development section helping to develop many of the important skills necessary for university and future life in a straight forward and understandable approach.*
*Most universities use the Harvard referencing system, this book displays different examples of this and lets you practise writing these for yourself; a very useful skill to learn as no doubt throughout university you will write hundreds of these in assignments and dissertations. It has also helped me develop my personal statement and CV to a high standard to prepare me for the future.*
*Before reading this book I would not have a clue how to write my CV and display the skills and achievements that I have earned through life at a high enough standard and format that employers expect. This book has enabled me to excel and fully develop the skills I have."*
*Postgraduate Student, Keele University.*

*"I thought it was pretty handy. I liked how simply it was written yet comprehensive in getting the message across."*
*Business student, Birmingham City University*

# Dedication and Thanks

**Dedication:**

I dedicate this book to my mum who passed away in 2000. Without her inspiration I would not have lead the life that I have, and have my mum's beliefs that

*"In life every goal is achievable, no matter what obstacles are put in the way.
You always get to where you want to be through hard work and determination."*

Thank you mum for this gift.

**I would like to say a big thank you to:**

Sally Wilson for your inspiration to write the book.
Margaret Greenhall for all your continued guidance and support and giving me the confidence to make writing the book so real.
Rob Ward at the Centre for Recording Achievement, for allowing me to present at the annual conference every year and promote good practice around other Universities in this country and the world.
Dr Evelyn Carnegie for allowing me the time to write and to use my resources that I have developed over the years.
My colleagues and friends for all their support and encouragement.
My little dog Bailey boy who has sat by me till every early hour of the morning whilst writing and preparing the book.
My daughter and granddaughter, Emma Louise and Ebony Mai, to whom the legacy will be left behind.
Finally, my mum who continues to inspire me every day to work hard to achieve the goals that I set for myself and those around me.

# About the Author:
# Angela Hepworth

Angela has over twenty years' experience teaching in Further and Higher Education. She is a Senior lecturer in the department of Sport and Physical Activity at Edge Hill University in Ormskirk, Lancashire specialising in personal and professional development and complementary therapies. She also specialises in life coaching.

Since the Dearing Report in 1997, Angela has been responsible for developing personal and professional development planning, working closely with other higher education institutes and the Centre for Recording Achievement (www.recordingachievement.org). Angela has presented her work at conferences and held workshops for staff and students around the country.

Angela has worked extensively with students to support them with developing their academic skills to help them pass their degrees. She encourages the students to work towards their goals, which will allow them to develop themselves personally and professionally, leading them to their chosen careers and dreams.

It is hoped that this book brings all aspects of personal development planning (PDP) together so students can build their portfolio and are able to showcase their work to prospective employers.

Angela has a daughter Emma Louise and a granddaughter Ebony Mai who inspire her to keep going. As well as lecturing at the university Angela travels all over the world as a guest lecturer on board cruise liners.

Angela's areas of expertise include:
- ✓ Personal and Professional Development
- ✓ Complementary Therapies
- ✓ Academic Skills
- ✓ Life Coaching
- ✓ Motivation Skills
- ✓ Inspiration Skills

# Contents

# List of Exercises

**Notes:**

# Chapter 1
# Introduction to Personal Development Planning

"The secret of getting ahead is getting started.
The secret of getting started is breaking your complex
overwhelming tasks into small manageable tasks,
and then starting on the first one." Mark Twain

# Chapter 1:
# Introduction to personal development planning

## What is personal development planning (PDP)?

*"Personal development planning is a structured and supported process to assist students in arranging their own personal educational and career progression." (Harvey, 2004)*

Personal development planning is a continuous programme of skills development. It puts control for learning into the hands of each student. It involves several processes:

✓ Recording your achievements in a portfolio (either paper or electronic)

✓ Thinking about your experiences and reflecting on how to improve for next time

✓ Understanding how you study and work and identifying how you could improve

✓ Planning your study

✓ Identifying and developing transferable skills to prepare for employment

✓ Identifying your dreams for your future

✓ Setting action goals to move you forward

In today's fast changing world people in all careers need to be able to plan their own learning to enhance and progress their career. PDP helps you to learn the skills to take control of your own progress right from the start. In the workplace the same process is often called continuous professional development (CPD) and is often part of the appraisal process.

14

## Background to the development of PDP

Since the Dearing Report (1997) and later the Burgess report (2007) personal development planning (PDP) (sometimes called progress files) has played a large part in students' lives. The government recommended that institutions of higher education identify opportunities to help students become familiar with work skills. They should also provide help for students to reflect on their learning experience. Students completing their degree programmes should have a clear understanding of key skills, communication, numeracy, the use of information technology and learning how to learn. Within postgraduate study research training should include the development of professional skills, such as communication, self-management and planning.

There has been confusion as to whose responsibility it is to deliver personal and professional development. In my view it is everyone's responsibility to ensure that the student has the best experiences possible whilst completing a learning programme. They should develop life long learning habits to carry them forward into the world of work.

It is up to academic staff and support services to provide opportunities to allow the student to:

✓ Gain the best possible degree classification
✓ Encourage the student to actively engage in the process to prepare them for employment

More and more employers are helping their employees to engage in continuous professional development (CPD) or lifelong learning. Companies and professional bodies often require people to continually update their professional skills. This process is assessed on an annual basis through staff appraisal and can sometimes be related to pay, conditions, supplementary bonuses and promotion.

This book aims to provide both staff and students with clearly defined examples that are easy to follow for the PDP process.

## The learning cycle:

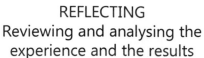

**EXPERIENCING**
Taking part in the
learning activity

**REFLECTING**
Reviewing and analysing the
experience and the results

**PLANNING**
Planning any changes
and new strategy

**THEORISING**
Integrating the experience with
both your own and
other people's views of the world

The above cycle is known as the Kolb or learning cycle. For effective learning people need to undertake all four parts. You need to take part in learning experiences, reflect on the experience and connect the experience to everything else you've learnt then plan your next learning experience. Traditionally degrees concentrated on helping people to learn the knowledge and skills needed for a particular career. Most courses had very little about the learning process itself and reflecting on how you learn and becoming a better learner. However, in the modern world, most people change careers several times. So you have to develop systems for coordinating your own personal development. Being able to reflect on your experience helps this process. PDP helps people to engage with all four parts of the learning cycle and so enhances careers.

# What do people say about Personal Development Planning?

## Academic staff comments

*"PDP is an essential element of the student experience in helping to develop the key skills and qualities that help students to successfully engage with their university course. It is also facilitates the awareness of and preparation for future career opportunities, helps raise their employability profile in the competitive job market. It fosters an appreciation of reflective practice and the benefits of continued professional development." Senior Lecturer*

*"Over the past nine years, that I have been involved with personal development planning, I have seen students have had to take their PDP more seriously. Students used to only see the relevance of PDP after they had completed the process in their final year. Now as the job market is even harder to get into and students know that graduate positions are hard to find, there has been a vast increase of first year students taking their PDP more seriously. They are looking at ways in which they can gain experience in their skills to be able to add to their curriculum vitae whilst they are in university. Also, students are undertaking more and more voluntary experience and degree enrichment to be able to offer this to industry when they apply for employment." Senior lecturer*

*Personal Development Planning, and the underlying activities that go to make it up - recording experiences and achievements, thinking about skills, values, attitudes, motivations, reflecting on experience, goal-setting and planning, summarising (for presentation to a third party), and above all understanding oneself as a learner - are key to successful learning and career development.*
*Rob Ward, Director, Centre for Recording Achievement*

**Students' comments**

*"At first I wasn't a big fan or believed it really wasn't relevant to me or my degree but over the duration of my course I now believe it to be essential for all students to do as it acts as a coping mechanism for all the stresses of being a student."*

*"It increased my knowledge of what an employer will be looking for as well as how I can tick those boxes."*

*"I found that the final year of PDP was really helpful as I began to apply for posts I felt confident and well prepared. In addition the feedback from my mock interview helped me to identify my strengths and weaknesses."*

*"Excellent skills for future jobs."*

*"I can search for jobs, create cover letters to employers, and I now know how to create a CV that should hopefully be a 'cut' above the rest. Without PDP I would not know what to do next with my future or how I can further develop myself."*

*"PDP is both relevant and useful."*

*"PDP gave me the resources to further my learning and allowed me to gain valuable skills that I will use in an everyday working environment."*

*"Through PDP I have learnt the skills appropriate for my job field and know how to act in a job setting. I believe PDP is good for identifying skills to be improved and used to further yourself in your career opportunities."*

*"I've found PDP very useful. The skills I've learnt will be used for years after the course is complete."*

*"A great way to raise awareness of the choices students have available to them after they finish their degree course. A good way to prepare students and give them good resources for further careers."*

*"PDP has helped to give me ideas as to the direction I want to follow in the future. In addition, I work shadowed an exercise referral specialist that not only helped me gain experience but also aided me in making my career decisions."*

# How to use this book

## Students:

This book has been designed to guide you through your course. You don't need to read it all the way through in one go. The best way to use it is to take a couple of minutes to look through each page at a rate of two seconds per page and evaluate the material and decide which bits you need now and flag up your in your mind what else is there for later. There are many exercises throughout the books and the idea is that as you reach the appropriate point in your course you do the exercise and add to your portfolio. Many of the exercises can be downloaded from www.uolearn.com as word documents so you can type directly into them and add them as either paper or electronic versions to your file.

**Staff:**

This book is designed to be a student friendly way to teach study and employability skills. The book is specially designed by an expert in reading to make it easy for your students to access and read. As such the writing style is fairly informal and friendly.

Many of the exercises can be downloaded and you are welcome to copy them for your class. There is also a tutor manual to accompany this book (available from June 2011, ISBN 978-1-84937-053-0) which can be ordered directly from either the study skills or shop part of www.uolearn.com.

For your students to order their own copies of the book please make sure you add it to your reading list and let your university book shop know in plenty of time to order it in for you. Also remember to get the library to get some copies in.

[Details for your book shop: Studying for Your Future, Angela Hepworth, ISBN  978-1-84937-047-9, our distributor is Bertrams.]

Students can also buy copies from any of the usual online bookshops such as Amazon and Waterstones. If you wish to order large numbers of copies for a library or your department please do contact the publisher directly (sales@uolearn.com). E-versions of the book are available from the publisher's website (www.uolearn.com) and the Kindle version from Amazon.

We welcome any feedback you have about the book and we are quite open to responding to suggested changes for the next version, if we feel it will help the students. (support@uolearn. com).

Finally, if you need help using any of the materials please do contact us and we'll try to do our best to come up with some suggestions.

## The structure of the book:

This book is divided into four main parts, following the skills development appropriate for each stage of university education.

Each section covers aspects of the PDP process in varying degrees of depth. There is no particular order to the different content within the process so you can use the book in any way that is appropriate to you.

Read it from cover to cover or take out of the book the parts that are relevant to you.

At the end of the book I have included resources and further reading that you may find useful to further your studies on each of the sections.

If you visit the website www.uolearn.com you will find free downloadable copies of most of the exercises from this book and plenty of space to write or type.

### Chapter 2: Year 1, starting your PDP

Chapter 2 aims at making you more employable by equipping you with the skills that employers are looking for and helping you to complete your degree programme. It enables you to look at how your degree programme fits together. It will help you to develop the skills you will need to complete your assignments and to prepare for your exams. Organising your time will play a significant role in making sure that you meet deadlines and have enough time to plan your assignments to carry out the appropriate research. This section will also help you to set achievable goals for yourself so that you can work towards these whilst completing your degree. The use of an assessment grid will allow you to see when all your assignments are due in and what dates you need to be aware of for assessment deadlines. This is the key to being successful on your degree programme.

### Chapter 3: Year 2, Skills Development

This section (chapter 3) helps you to develop the skills you will need when you become an employee. It will also help you to reflect on the first year of your degree so that you can prepare yourself to achieve high grades for your degree classification.

This section will allow you to complete a SWEAT analysis (see chapter 3) so that you can identify what areas you need to improve or maintain in order to keep you on track. The additional skills that you will develop from this section will include problem solving, motivating others, effective team working and leadership skills.

### Chapters 4 and 5: Years 2 and 3, Preparing for Work

The aim of chapter 4 and 5 is to prepare you to leave university and help you to enter your chosen career. It will also allow you to update your curriculum vitae in a format that is acceptable to employers. If you are undecided where you want to work when you leave university, this section will take you through a series of questions which will allow you to question the environment you want to be part of, the people you want to work with and what you are really interested in doing.

Job websites are also provided in this section so that you can start to look at what is potentially out there. You will be able to find out how to make contact with employers so that you can have a head start before you finish your degree programme. It also provides you with sample letters to apply for employment or ask for placement opportunities.

This section aims to get you thinking about your research and where you want to go with your study, whether you want to take it further into master's study or to write a journal article or present at a conference and how you can go about doing this.

This year you may be asked to present your work with a viva (oral presentation) and there are suggestions on what to include in your presentation.

There is advice to help you get ready for interviews, decide what to wear, present yourself and also think about the type of questions which could be asked.

# Checklist for the contents of your PDP portfolio

You need to collect evidence for your development portfolio to give you evidence of your skills development. It will also help you to remember what you've done and to track your own progress. Here is a suggested list of the contents of your portfolio. Many of the items will be described in much more details later in the book.

- ❑ Personal statement
- ❑ Reflections on your experiences
- ❑ Stories of your successes
- ❑ Action plans
- ❑ Time management study
- ❑ Your priorities
- ❑ Weekly planners
- ❑ Your dreams
- ❑ Short/mid/long term goals
- ❑ Revisiting your goals
- ❑ Assessment grid for all your modules
- ❑ Feedback on your assignments
- ❑ Examples of assignments that you're proud of
- ❑ Example of your lecture notes

23

# CHECKLIST FOR YOUR PORTFOLIO

- ☐ Plan for an essay/lab report/assignment
- ☐ Plan for a presentation
- ☐ Feedback on a presentation
- ☐ Examples of critical thinking
- ☐ Referencing list
- ☐ A literature review
- ☐ A list of all the activities you did outside of your studies
- ☐ A list of any responsibilities you had
- ☐ Grades, estimated and achieved
- ☐ SWEAT analysis
- ☐ Skills review (problem solving, motivating others, team working, leadership, other skills)
- ☐ Evidence of your careers searches
- ☐ Your ideal working life
- ☐ A list of the contact details of possible employers
- ☐ A great CV
- ☐ An outline of any research project you did
- ☐ Your presentation of your research project
- ☐ An example application form
- ☐ Letters for applications
- ☐ Your thoughts on typical interview questions

**Notes:**

**Notes:**

# Chapter 2
# Year 1, starting your PDP

"Planning is bringing the future into the present so that you can do something about it now." Alan Lakein

# Chapter 2:
# Year 1, starting your PDP

## Getting organised and understanding yourself

You are going to be undertaking many exercises that form a portfolio for you to monitor and reflect on your progress. You need to decide whether you are going to store this electronically or on paper.

### On paper:

Get a large ring binder and buy some dividers and plastic wallets to store your materials.

### On computer:

You may need a scanner as many of the things you might like to include may be initially paper based. Create a folder for each main topic. Many universities now have electronic versions of PDP within their intranet.

Exercise 1: Getting organised for PDP

Choose how you are going to record your portfolio and organise your filing system. Start collecting any materials that you think will help you demonstrate your skills.

## Personal Statement

In order to get you started with your personal development planning, it is important that your personal tutor gets to know who you are and what your needs are for the programme. Often your personal tutor will be someone who is part of your subject area. It is important to carry out the following exercise as it helps everyone. It will also give you a starting point to come back to and consider when you are further along in your studies. This task is always better hand written so that you can 'free write' whatever comes into your mind.

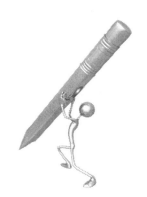

This exercise will give the reader of your portfolio some background information about you. It will give them an idea about your writing style, whether you have any problems around grammar, punctuation, dyslexia and dyspraxia which may lead to further problems for you with your study. The more you write the easier it becomes when you allow your mind to become creative.

If you already have a diagnosis of needing special support it is vital that you let the university know as soon as you can. Most universities have specialist centres to help with things like dyslexia and can provide a wider range of help than your school might have done.

Exercise 2: Write a short paragraph on each of the following:

Who are you?

...................................................................................................

...................................................................................................

...................................................................................................

...................................................................................................

...................................................................................................

Where are you from?

...................................................................................................

...................................................................................................

...................................................................................................

...................................................................................................

Describe your family.

...................................................................................................

...................................................................................................

...................................................................................................

...................................................................................................

Write about your previous studies.

...................................................................................................

...................................................................................................

...................................................................................................

...................................................................................................

...................................................................................................

Why did you choose this course and college or university?

What do you hope to achieve from your degree programme?

What type of jobs would you like to apply for when you complete your degree programme?

## Reflection

Throughout your life and also your degree programme you will go through different experiences that you may need to reflect upon. You may be asked to write a reflective log, a reflective report or to write down the thoughts you went through whilst progressing through a certain experience. This may mean that you have to look back on the process that you went through and then decide what you would do if you were to go through a similar process again.

### Questions for reflection:

✓ What did you do?

✓ Would you go through the process in exactly the same way if you did something similar in the future?

✓ What did you learn from carrying out the process in the way that you did?

✓ What advice would you give yourself if you had to go through the process again?

Reflective practice, reflective practitioner, reflective log, reflective action plan, reflective diary and reflective journal; these are all key words that allow the writer to write in the first person. "I did this." 'I felt this." You need to describe both what happened and describe how it made you feel and how you would approach the same issue again.

This kind of writing is different from academic writing which doesn't allow you to write in the first person, you may only write in the third person (he/she/Mr Smith etc.).

You may be asked as part of your course to keep a reflective log or journal which you may write in everyday or every week for a short or long period of time.

You may also be asked to contribute to an online blog or discussion page which a select group have been invited to join. This is a good way to share experiences and challenges that you may be having. You can support each other and help to alleviate tension or problems when reading other people's reflective journals.

Exercise 3: Choose a recent experience you had, maybe learning to drive or taking your exams:

What did you do?

..........................................................................................................

..........................................................................................................

..........................................................................................................

..........................................................................................................

Would you go through the process in exactly the same way if you did something similar in the future?

..........................................................................................................

..........................................................................................................

..........................................................................................................

..........................................................................................................

What did you learn from carrying out the process in the way that you did?

..........................................................................................................

..........................................................................................................

..........................................................................................................

..........................................................................................................

What advice would you give yourself if you had to go through the process again?

..........................................................................................................

..........................................................................................................

..........................................................................................................

..........................................................................................................

## Action Planning

To keep your life in some kind of order it is important to have achievable goals and also to create action plans. Planning and goal setting will help you to become more successful in your study and career.

It is important when you get your first assignment that you devise an action plan to state how you are going to fit in the time to do your research, reading, writing, typing, checking and complete all the referencing part of your work. This can sometimes be the most time consuming part of your project/assignment.

As well as all the other commitments it is important to write an action plan which will help you to stay on track with completing a task. When you have finished your action plan, add into your dairy the commitments it involves.

It is a good way to practise your time management skills to reach the deadlines and targets set on your degree programme or projects within your workplace.

Following are some examples of an academic and non-academic action plans.

**Action plan to complete a 2,000 word assignment.**

Title of assignment:

Date to be completed: Thurs 24th March

| Time scale | Action | Key points | Date completed | Notes |
|---|---|---|---|---|
| Week 1<br><br>Start date:<br><br>Mon 28th Feb | Go to library for key reading take out relevant books.<br>Print off the journal articles.<br><br>Write plan for assignment. | Some books are only on 1 week loan. Read first and return.<br>Show plan to tutor in next seminar. | | |
| Week 2<br><br>Date: Mon 7th March<br><br>Weds/Fri and Sunday afternoon. | Write introduction.<br>Start reading books and articles for key literature and quotes to back up arguments.<br>Aim to write 500 words. | Ask Ben if we can go out on Tues not Weds so I can work through into the evening. | | |
| Week 3<br><br>Date: Mon 14th March<br><br>Mon/Thurs and Sat | Write main body of the assignment.<br>Aim to write 1000 words. | Working Tues, Weds, Fri so will only have Mon and Thurs evenings free. Go to bed straight after shifts at 10. | | |
| Week 4:<br><br>Date: Mon 21st March | Write summary.<br>Read through and check it answers the question.<br>Check for errors and make corrections.<br>Hand in on 24th. | | | |

ACTION PLANNING

**Action plan to apply for a new job.**

Title of job:

Company:

Address:

Date to be completed: Friday 15th July (due date Thurs 21st)

| Time scale | Action | Key points | Date completed | Notes |
|---|---|---|---|---|
| Mon 27th June | Ask for application form | Check if you can submit electronically and what other data they need. Find out if there is an interview date set. | | |
| Mon 4th/ Tues 5th July | Research company on internet. Rewrite CV | | | |
| Weds 6th | Check references are up to date, send emails or tel to ask permission to use their names. Write personal statement. | Seeing personal tutor on Monday - ask them then if I can use as a referee. | | |
| Sat 9th | Fill in application form. | Make a photocopy and check spacings work before filling in the real one. | | |
| Weds 13th | Write covering letter. Proofread all materials. | Ask Louise if she'll have a quick look as she is great at proofreading. | | |
| Fri 15th | Post form | Do it at the post office to get it right. | | |

Follow up action plan:

| Did you get an interview?<br>Date:<br>Place:<br>Type: | Yes/no |
|---|---|
| If not get some feedback | Key points to act on next time: |
| 1 | |
| 2 | |
| 3 | |
| 4 | |
| 5 | |

**Case Study: Getting first class honours**

Peter was in his final year of study and realised very early on that he was on line for a 2:1 degree. He also knew that if he really worked hard he could achieve a first class honours degree. If he worked closely with his dissertation supervisor then he could really do well and achieve a high grade.
This motivated Peter, so early on in his final year of study he completed an action plan which included all the tasks he had to do for his dissertation. He set his action plan so that there were certain tasks he had to complete. Knowing he only had twelve weeks to carry out research, he had to get it right.

Here are some of the things he had on his action plan: firstly have his research ethically approved; provide a literature review; write up his methodology and analyse all of the data he was going to collect. He discussed the action plan with his dissertation supervisor and took the action plan along to every meeting so that he could show his tutor that he was on track, or if he was a little behind he could seek help. This process benefited Peter enormously and he commented that without the action plan his research would not have followed a plan, and he would have been totally disorganised.

Exercise 4: Action planning

Complete an action plan for an aspect of your course, this could be an assignment, revision, team activity, job application, a project etc.

You can download blank versions of this grid from www.uolearn.com.

**Action plan for:**

Date to start:

Date to be completed:

| Time scale | Action | Key points | Date complete | Notes |
|---|---|---|---|---|
| | | | | |
| | | | | |
| | | | | |
| | | | | |
| | | | | |
| | | | | |

## Time Management

When we think about how much time can be wasted being non-productive, it is important that we plan our time effectively. Particularly, when you are doing a degree programme and you have deadlines to meet as well as juggling busy social lives and part time jobs and family.

One thing that is important to realise is that when there are too many things on the to-do list it is virtually impossible to stay focused.

### Here are ten time saving suggestions:

✓ Adopt mindmapping or concept maps (see later) for all your notes taken in lectures

✓ Save time by reading weeks in advance the materials you need for your assignments

✓ Keep your notes in one particular place to avoid having to look through pages and pages of subject material

✓ Use a word limit to focus your energies

✓ Avoid duplicating effort

✓ Action plan each assignment

✓ Action plan your exam revision timetable

✓ Action plan your week

✓ Set yourself a daily goal

✓ Everyday say to yourself...... The purpose of the day is.......

39

**Managing your time:**

➢ Be aware of your own time management

➢ Make a note of how much time it takes you to complete each type of study task

➢ Take into account that many aspects of study take longer than expected

➢ Schedule time for unforeseen events

➢ Schedule time for relaxation and leisure

### Exercise 5: Workflow diary

Many people just do not know how long it takes them to complete simple repetitive tasks.

Either:

Keep a diary for 3 days noting how long you take to do everything.
or
Add any more tasks you can think of then time the following list, you'll be amazed how long things take.

| Task | Time (mins) |
|---|---|
| Make a hot drink | |
| Read 10 pages of a typical text book | |
| Type 200 words | |
| Find a useful website about one of your recent lectures | |
| Travel to a class | |
| Do your grocery shopping | |
| | |
| | |
| | |
| | |

Exercise 6: How well do you manage your time?

Rate yourself on a scale of 1:awful to 5:excellent for the following:

| | 1 | 2 | 3 | 4 | 5 |
|---|---|---|---|---|---|
| Do you usually turn up on time? | ☹ | ○ | ☺ | ○ | ☺ |
| Do you keep most appointments? | ☹ | ○ | ☺ | ○ | ☺ |
| Do you manage to fit in most of the things that you need to do? | ☹ | ○ | ☺ | ○ | ☺ |
| Do you get most things done without a last minute panic? | ☹ | ○ | ☺ | ○ | ☺ |
| Do you meet dead lines? | ☹ | ○ | ☺ | ○ | ☺ |
| Do you set time aside to relax? | ☹ | ○ | ☺ | ○ | ☺ |
| Do you use your time efficiently? | ☹ | ○ | ☺ | ○ | ☺ |
| Do you get on with tasks as soon as you get them? | ☹ | ○ | ☺ | ○ | ☺ |
| Can you find things quickly on your desk? | ☹ | ○ | ☺ | ○ | ☺ |
| Did you get everything done you needed to last week? | ☹ | ○ | ☺ | ○ | ☺ |
| Do you keep your diary up to date? | ☹ | ○ | ☺ | ○ | ☺ |
| **Total** | | | | | |

Add up your total score:

10-25, you need to seriously look at your time management - you're working very inefficiently. You need to reappraise how you work and write an action plan for change. Each week pick one area of time management to work on, maybe decluttering your work environment or making a system for meeting your deadlines.

26-45, You're not working very efficiently and there is room for improvement. Pick 2 things from the list and work on them over the next week.

46-55, You've got great time management skills.

**Procrastination**

Are you avoiding working?

Have you found yourself cleaning out the bottom drawer of your cupboard?

Avoiding a task will increase the size of your activation energy to start it. If you find you're doing lots of make work things like dusting your plants then you're avoiding something bigger.

The way to tackle a big task is to break it down into lots of smaller, more manageable tasks. For any task you have to do write down all the components (if you have tasks that are repeated often, like writing an essay keep hold of this list). This is now a closed list and is much easier to work with than a to-do list because it never grows bigger and you can have a sense of completion as you tick off the individual components. A to-do list never finishes, there is always something else to add to it. Don't think about doing the whole assignment; just make it your goal to do one of the very small tasks. It doesn't matter which one, you've got to eventually do it all anyway so start with the one you'll find easiest to do.

You can also trick yourself by saying, "All I'm going to do is just open the file. Then all I'm going to do is write one sentence." Make it something you couldn't possibly fail to complete.

If you're still finding it hard to start then make yourself work for 5 minutes only and no more. How hard could it be to just tap away at your keyboard for 5 minutes? Even if it's no good and you delete it later at least you've started on your journey.

Once you start you'll find you want to continue.

*"You can do anything for 5 minutes!" Mark Forster*

Work with your own time patterns. Are you a morning or late night person? Choose tasks to fit with your most alert times.

A tip is that most people's attention span for not very exciting stuff is 20 minutes so think about working for 15 minutes then change to a different task.

## Your Work Environment

It is really important to choose your work environment very carefully as you may work better in one room rather than another. It may be that you can only work well in a library atmosphere. Make sure you choose a place where you can avoid distraction. You must have comfort for your back, legs and shoulders, somewhere warm and somewhere you have access to drinking and toilet facilities.

A very important aspect of time management is to make sure your work environment is organised. If your desk is cluttered and disorganised not only will you waste time but also you'll get into a bad mood hunting for your stapler for the 2001st time this week. Some people like to have everything neat and filed away all the time, others need to see all of what they are working on at once. If you are one of the latter then make sure you have a large pen pot or set of in-trays for all your equipment like stapler, blue tack etc. and get into the habit of using them and returning them. Once a week or at the end of each major assignment clear your desk and tidy everything up.

Andrew is a mature student in his final year of study who also runs a very successful training consultancy. His ultimate goal in life is to become a university lecturer. Andrew realised that this final year was going to be the most trying out of all the years at University. He had to combine family life, running his consultancy and also all the pressures of completing his degree to a really high standard in order to then go on to doing a master's, then PhD and then finally to teaching. Andrew needed to sit down and complete a time management plan as he was worried that there was nowhere in his weekly schedule that he could physically fit in a day's study to concentrate on his dissertation and other assignments and projects he had to juggle to meet deadlines. When he went through the time management plan, he realised that he could move his consultancy work around to suit his studies. He decided, just for a few weeks, to rely more heavily on his staff. He knew that this would not be a permanent arrangement. Once the plan was completed he knew exactly what he should be working on every day and this gave him more focus.

## Getting Organised For Your Study

Before you started at university you would have been given access to reading lists and module booklets for the modules you are going to be studying. The reading lists are the recommended reading you should read to contribute to group discussions, lectures, workshops and to help you to complete your assignments. Books can be an expensive resource so you may want to check the notice boards around the university to see if there are any students selling their books that they no longer use. Some websites and student unions have used books for sale too.

Print off journal articles ready for your assignment and file them in separate box files with the module code on the side, so you know where everything is for that module. This way you will be able to go to the module box when you are writing up your assignments and have all your information organised. It is also a good idea to go through the articles and highlight the relevant and most important statements as well as the references and keep records of where you found each piece of information.

Get organised with files for your study either a file for every day or a file module by module so that you know exactly where all your notes are. You will need a separate file for your personal development portfolio. The tasks within this book can be downloaded and either completed electronically or printed off and handwritten. This will allow you to build a portfolio to enable you to give specific examples of how you have developed your skills to potential employers.

Your university may have an electronic portfolio system that they may want you to use, this may be in the form of blogs, Moodle, Pebblepad, Blackboard etc.

Exercise 7: Time planning - prioritising

Draw up a priority setting checklist:

1.  Write a list of everything you have to do.
2.  Underline essential tasks in one colour and items that can wait in another colour.
3.  Identify the most urgent item on the list.
4.  Work out the best way this task can be approached.
5.  Only focus on that one essential item, the rest can wait, otherwise you will bombard your brain and not achieve anything.
6.  Work out how long you can spend on the urgent item to get the task completed before you can move onto the next task on your list.
7.  Enter each essential task into your timetable or diary.
8.  Avoid the things that take away your concentration levels, such as internet, television, mobile phone or other people. Music can help concentration but not if you're shouting out the words to the song!

| Task | Priority |
| --- | --- |
|  |  |
|  |  |
|  |  |
|  |  |
|  |  |
|  |  |
|  |  |
|  |  |
|  |  |
|  |  |
|  |  |
|  |  |
|  |  |

## Exercise 8: Time planning - weekly planner

Another good way to plan out your time is to draw up a timetable of the week with 7 rows 3 columns. You can also buy diaries that have a week to view on a two page spread.

Fill the timetable in with everything that you do in your life for one week and see where you can free up some time to fit in study and revision time.

Obviously if you have to work part time as well you can't change the time that you go to work. You will then be able to see a pattern emerging that you tend to get some free time maybe on a Saturday or a Sunday afternoon.

|  | Morning | Afternoon | Evening |
|---|---|---|---|
| Monday |  |  |  |
| Tuesday |  |  |  |
| Wednesday |  |  |  |
| Thursday |  |  |  |
| Friday |  |  |  |
| Saturday |  |  |  |
| Sunday |  |  |  |

## Goal Setting

If you don't know where you are going, how do you ever expect to get there!!!!

In everything that we do in life we must set clear achievable goals for ourselves.

These may be short term, medium term or long term.

A short term goal may be achievable in one day, one week or one month.

A medium term goal may be achieved over a period of two to six months and long term goals are usually over a period of six months to ten years.

Inspirational speakers and writers worldwide talk about goal setting and focusing in on the energy to achieve that goal. My life coach once said to me that if you want to achieve a goal you have to do something about it every day. Chip, chip, chip away and you will get there I promise you.

Examples to inspire you may be:

✓ Starting your own business
✓ Improving your writing skills
✓ Becoming a professional footballer
✓ Becoming a better coach
✓ Becoming a newsreader
✓ Travelling the world
✓ Achieving your degree
✓ Undertake some management training
✓ Learn to organise time more efficiently
✓ Finish master's degree
✓ Learn yoga
✓ Go to the gym three times a week
✓ Eat more healthily
✓ Write a menu plan for the week so that my eating is healthier and not always prepared in a rush

~~~
**Case study: Life time achievements**

When he was 15, John Goddard wrote a list of 127 dreams to achieve in his life. It wasn't just ordinary things there were some things that seemed impossible at the time (it was written in 1940) and included a visit to the moon. He has accomplished 109 out of that list. Including:

Explore: the Nile, the Amazon and the Congo rivers.

Climb: Mt Kenya, Mt Rainer, Mt Fuji

Photograph: Victoria falls, Yosemite falls,

Retrace the steps of Marco Pole and Alexander the Great

Visit: The Great Wall of China, Easter Island, The Taj Mahal

Swim in: Lake Superior, Lake Victoria, Lake Nicaragua

Accomplish: Write a book, Publish in National Geographic, Run a mile in 5 mins, Learn French, Spanish and Arabic, Make a telescope, Watch a cremation ceremony in Bali, Marry and have children, Land off and take off from an aircraft carrier, Circumnavigate the globe.

To see the full list visit: http://www.johngoddard.info/life_list.htm
~~~

Goals differ from dreams in that they are based on your knowledge of where you are and the journey you can definitely travel. Dreams are what you can achieve in your lifetime but you may not currently have the equipment to start the journey.

Examples:

Goals: Complete my essay by next Monday.
To get a first class honours degree.

Dreams: To walk on Mars.
To fly across the country in a hot air balloon.

**Exercise 9: What are your dreams?**

What if you had completely unlimited money?
What will you really love to have done by the time you're 80?

Date:

49

Exercise 10: Goal setting

Take some time out of your busy schedule to think about some goals you would like to set for yourself.
These should be SMART

Specific - you can identify exactly what to do.

Measurable - you'll know when you've finished.

Achievable - you have or can get the resources.

Relevant - they are relevant to your larger goals.

Time - they have a time for completion.

|  | Short term goal                Date: |
|---|---|
| Today | |
| This week | |
| Next 30 days | |

| | Medium term goals | Date: |
|---|---|---|
| Two months time | | |
| Three months time | | |

| | Long term goals | Date: |
|---|---|---|
| 1 year | | |
| 2 years | | |
| 5 years | | |

## Assessment and Module Planning

Every module that you undertake at university will have an assessment of some form during or at the end of the module. Usually the first year of your degree programme doesn't count towards your overall degree classification. So, you can use the first year of your degree to learn how to plan your studies and have a practice at achieving high grades, which you can then improve on for the second and third year of your degree.

So many students go through University or College without any time planning, goal setting or preparation for assessment and their marks suffer because of this.

Usually on your university website you can find the module outlines. If they are not on the web ask at the department office to see a copy or they may be stored in the library. The module documents will tell you not only what the assessment strategy is but also the curriculum. They are not going to be exciting reading but think of them as insider knowledge. If you've read the module document you'll know the syllabus that should be covered. This means you could start to read ahead of the sessions. Now the module documents won't have the exact dates for your year so you'll have to either ask if there is an overall assignment schedule or ask each individual lecturer for the due dates of their assignments. When you have completed your assessment grid you can put a copy of it on your notice board or in your diary so that you can see exactly when work is due in. You need to do this at the start of every semester.

It is important at the start of every module that you complete an assessment grid. You can then work out an action plan if the module assessment is an assignment or exams, course work or projects that require time for preparation. From each individual module you can then construct a term planner (get an annual wall planner from a stationery shop). Following is an example of an assessment grid.

**Assessment Grid**

| Module title | Psychology | Notes/marks |
|---|---|---|
| Module code | PY105 | |
| Credits | 30 | |
| Module leader | John Smith | |
| My lecturers | Betty Brown<br>Peter Pen | Mainly Dr Brown |
| **Assessment** | **Date** | |
| 1 x 2000 word essay (35%) | 15th Nov | 62 % (21.7) |
| 1 x 2 hour exam (35%) | 10th Jan | 42 % (14.7) |
| 1 x 30 min group presentation (30%) | Week starting 3rd Dec | 55 % (16.5) |
| | **Overall mark** | 48% |
| Other:<br>Assessment feedback<br>Assignment feedback | 21st Jan<br>21st Jan | Feedback: On exam I didn't have time for question 4, which was worth 20% so Dr Brown was quite pleased with my knowledge but says I need to work on my time management in exams. |

The numbers in the right hand column in brackets are the marks times the percentage for that assignment divided by 100 (eg. (62x35)/100 = 21.7). These will then add up to your overall module mark. Be warned, this may be out by 1-2 % from your actual recorded mark as the rounding may work differently in the official spreadsheet.

## Exercise 11: Your module assessment grid

Complete an assessment grid for all your modules that you will study this year. This will help you to become focused and organised.

Remember you can download more forms from www.uolearn.com

| Module title | | Notes/marks |
|---|---|---|
| Module code | | |
| Credits | | |
| Module leader | | |
| My lecturers | | |
| **Assessment** | **Date** | **Marks** |
| | | |
| | | |
| | | |
| | | |
| | **Overall mark** | |
| Other: | | |

## Assessment Criteria Explained

Every piece of work that you have to complete as part of your degree programme will have an assessment criteria. This is a set of statements that will categorise which classification your piece of work will be awarded. A member of the academic team decides on the assessment criteria when they write the module document.

This will usually be a grid with mark ranges relating to degree classification and the set of criteria needed to achieve that grade. Within the table will then be a set of statements that your assignments will fit into.

On the next page there is an excerpt showing just some of the categories for the assessment criteria for a PDP module.

It is important that you read the assessment criteria before you start your assignment as this will tell you exactly how this piece of work will be marked and you will be able to match your work to the criteria and probably guess what grade your tutor will award before you hand it in.

Sometimes it is a good idea to read your assignment out loud to someone who knows nothing about your subject. Then you will know if it reads correctly and you can also check if you have commas, full stops and paragraphs in all the right places. Another way is to get your fellow students to peer review your work so that they award it with a mark. [A peer is someone with a similar level of skills to you.]

Once you have received your mark back from your tutor you should be able to then reflect on the feedback and make some notes on how you may improve for the next time.

You may also wish to book an appointment with your module tutor to ask how you might improve your grade.

Reflection is important otherwise you will carry on making the same mistakes and receiving the same grade.

## ASSESSMENT CRITERIA

Level 1: Developing Academic and Personal Skills Portfolio Assessment Criteria (partial table only, from 1 university, others will differ)

| | I (70-79%) | Fail (39-26%) |
|---|---|---|
| **Portfolio Tasks**<br><br>Completeness of the portfolio including appropriate coverage, focus and progression of specific tasks set | Excellent coverage of all of the tasks set, high level of synthesis of material with good progression, good focus on the material presented. | Basic coverage of the some of the tasks set but the file is incomplete, limited synthesis of material with little appropriate evidence of progression, limited focus on the material presented. |
| **Research Skills**<br><br>Evidence of appropriate research skills to approach both familiar and unfamiliar situations | Evidence within the portfolio demonstrates a high level of research skills. | Evidence within the portfolio demonstrates a limited level of research skills. |
| **Key and Transferable Skills**<br><br>Evidence of appropriate key and transferable skills including communication, numeracy, ICT and problem solving | Evidence within the portfolio demonstrates a high level of key and transferable skills. | Evidence within the portfolio demonstrates a limited level of key and transferable skills. |
| **General**<br><br>Appropriate format, appropriate writing style, conciseness, grammar and sentence structure. Format and layout of portfolio | Presentation, sentence structure, grammar and spelling are wholly acceptable, clear and coherent writing style, clear and concise structure that was easy to follow, high level of comprehensibility | Presentation, sentence structure, grammar and spelling are below an acceptable standard, negligible evidence of an appropriate writing style little discernible structure, a largely inappropriate level of comprehensibility. |

Students are not renowned for collecting the feedback on their assignments; they are only interested in the grade. Lecturers spend hours and hours marking, writing or typing up feedback, so it is important when you receive your feedback or mark that you book an appointment with the tutor so that you can discuss the feedback for next time you write. You will increase your grades by reflecting on your feedback. Ask advice from your tutors to identify where you could have improved and if you were to carry out a piece of work next time what would be the best advice to increase the grade.

---

### Exercise 12: Assignment Feedback

As part of your development collect all your assignment feedback sheets and look at the common themes that your tutors are saying about your assignments. Make a list of the common themes, these may be negative/constructive as well as positive e.g. not enough references, excellent referencing, good structure, poor layout, not enough reading, too much material. If you need help you may be able to book an appointment with a study advisor.

| Advice on improvement | What did I do right? |
|---|---|
|  |  |

---

## Taking Effective Lecture Notes

It is important for you to turn up to your lecture well prepared. Make sure you have with you a pen, pencil and paper or electronic gadget to take notes. To make really useful notes a range of coloured pens is a good idea as you can then colour code different aspects of the lecture. The best ones are the fineliners. Your lecturer may allow you to take in your lap top or smart phone so that you can take notes directly onto them.

It is a good idea to always write down the main title of the lecture and the date. This will help you to identify your notes later.

It is important that you listen carefully to what is being said so that you can pick out the points that will be key for you to remember. Don't try to write everything down that is being presented as before you know it the lecturer is on to the next slide and you are mid sentence missing the main point.

Sometimes the lecturer will provide the lecture slides before the lecture so that you may print off the notes beforehand and make notes alongside what is being said. Notes should be taken in every lecture whether the lecturer provides handouts or not. Your own thoughts on the material will help you to understand the material much better than the printed handouts.

In terms of both understanding and remembering the lecture it is important to make connections with the rest of the information you have in your brain. A good lecturer will help you do this with examples and stories of how the information can be used but you must always be alert and make your own connections. The best way to do this is to set yourself questions that help flag up important points as you listen.

### Before the lecture

Briefly remind yourself of any connecting lectures by looking through your previous notes or handouts. Download and read any lecture notes that have been provided. Set yourself a specific question that you need answering about the probable content of the upcoming lecture. Write this under the title of the lecture.

**During the lecture:**
- ➢ Listen for the answer to your specific question.
- ➢ What's the story behind the theory?
- ➢ How does this lecture connect to your previous studies?
- ➢ How could you use the information being given?
- ➢ Is any of it relevant to possible exam questions?
- ➢ How could it be applied to a different situation?
- ➢ Which idea is the lecturer emphasising?
- ➢ What 5 key words would summarise the lecture?
- ➢ Can you draw an image of what the lecture means to you?

In your notes use a different colour for important points, specific quotes or formulae. Develop your own colour coding system to use in all your lectures.

If you don't understand something ask straight away, if possible, and if not ask either the lecturer or your friends at the end. One principle that the best students have is they don't leave until they understand everything.

One of the best ways to take notes in lecture is through drawing yourself a concept map, mindmap or spider diagram (see below). You can download free mindmapping software quite easily. You can also get a free booklet on mindmapping from www. UoLearn.com.

**After the lecture:**
- ➢ Re-read your notes and add to them within 24 hours of the session
- ➢ If there are still points you don't understand then follow them up on the internet, library, with friends or write them down as questions to ask when you have a tutorial
- ➢ File your notes away systematically so that you can easily find them
- ➢ Make sure you follow up on any suggested reading
- ➢ Practise using any practical information like analysis techniques before the next lecture so that you can check you've understood them

**An example of a mindmap** (See www.uolearn.com to see it in detail and colour.)

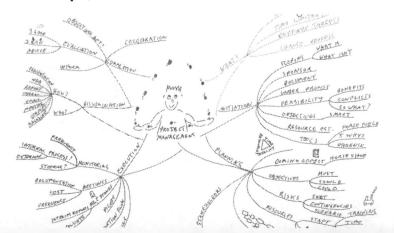

**An example of a concept map:**

Similar concepts are shown using the same shapes or colours and more detail is usually given than a mindmap.

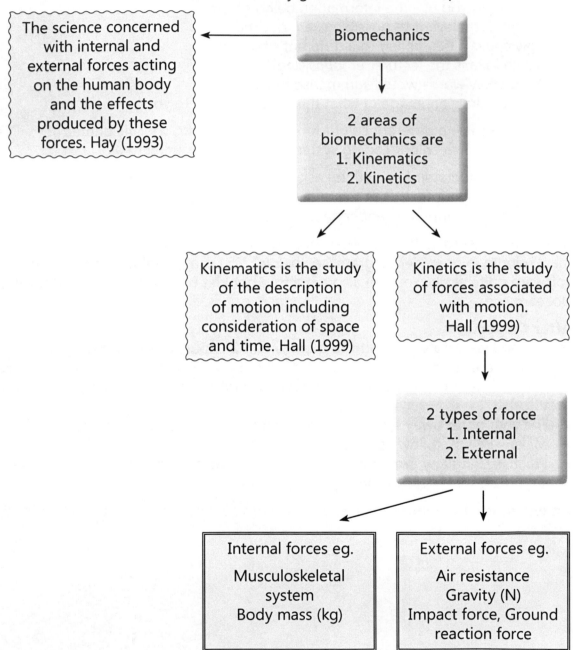

Exercise 13: Mind and Concept Mapping

Using a set of lecture notes produce a mind map or concept map relevant to your studies. Choose any topic from any lecture. You may want to use this when you come to revise for your final exams.

I always advise students to start in the centre of the page with the title of the lecture and then work outwards with notes and ideas.

# Essay Planning and Writing

Do you have anxieties about writing? By the end of this section you will be able to stop your mind from becoming empty and know where to begin with your essay or project.

**So how do you do all this?**

✓ Firstly you need to clarify the task before you start researching, know what you are looking for, by examining the title and course notes really carefully. Find out exactly what is required; ask your tutor early on if you are unsure.

✓ Write one line to sum up your basic opinion or argument. Adapt it as you proceed.

✓ Produce a mind map or a concept map to record what you know.

✓ Decide what you need to read or find out.

✓ Collect and record information.

✓ Get the information you need but be focused, be selective-you can't use everything.

✓ Write a set of questions to guide your research and look for the answers.

✓ Check the word limit to see how much information you can use for each point, and keep a notebook nearby to jot down all your ideas.

✓ As you go through your research keep on asking yourself, "Do I need this information, and if so how will I use it?

✓ You need to record information as you go along stating where you found the information and ideas for your reference list.

✓ Make a note of themes, theories, dates, data, names, explanations, examples, details, evidence and page numbers, as you go along as you will find it difficult to do this at the end of your essay.

**When you have gathered the information, think about you have discovered.**

➤ Has your viewpoint changed?
➤ Have you clarified your argument?
➤ Have you enough evidence /examples?
➤ What arguments or evidences oppose your point of view?
➤ Are they valid?
➤ Is it clearer to you why this task was set?

When you are writing your outline plan and first draft you need to work out the order to introduce your ideas, using your mind map, concept map or headings and points. Work out how many words you can write on each point, and don't be frightened of writing your first draft, start with whatever seems the easiest, just keep on writing, you will soon get into the flow. Don't worry about the style of your writing for now. To begin with just clearly state things and use simple short sentences.

Write out the title on a piece of paper in large handwriting so that you stay focused on the title when you are writing, so many students go off on a tangent and don't end up answering the question.

Underline the key words you are being asked to write about, describe, analyse, compare, contrast, explain...........

> **Case Study: Learning to write**
>
> In the first six weeks of starting university Julian was asked to write a 1,000 word assignment which had to be submitted using the correct layout for the assignment. It had to include referencing from at least four books, three journal articles, a government report or policy, two newspapers and three relevant websites. This was quite a daunting task for Julian as he had never written in the third person before. He was used to writing descriptively using the words 'I think this because of that'. Now he had to start to learn how to write more academically using the words 'Various studies suggest that'. This was difficult for Julian at first but he learnt how to progress with his skills by having regular appointments with his personal tutor and asking for feedback. The most important skill that he learnt was that reading was the key to writing. The more he read the more he understood how the academics wrote their articles and so he adopted the same style.

**Verbs used in assignment titles**

| Verb | Interpretation |
|---|---|
| Account for | Explain why something happened |
| Account of | Describe the order in which events happened |
| Analyse | Break the topic down into smaller parts and show how they relate to each other, look for patterns |
| Assess | Consider all aspects that contribute, positive and negative, and then decide how important it was |
| Compare | Take 2 or more components and write about the same aspect for each one to find out what they have in common and how they differ. |
| Contrast | Same as compare but concentrate more on the differences. |
| Define | List the aspects which make that issue unique from all others, explain what it means. |
| Describe | Give the relevant attributes of the issue, if physical it would be size, colour etc. if an event it could be the date, location, people involved etc. |
| Discuss | Debate the pros and cons of a situation |
| Evaluate | Same as assess |
| Explain | Give the reasons behind a situation, the causes and effects |
| To what extent, How far | Similar to assess but usually implies the reason given isn't the whole issue and is looking to you to give other explanations and weigh up which is the biggest influence. |
| Illustrate | Give specific examples |
| List | Similar to describe |
| Relate | Same as compare |
| Review | Go over the background and pull together various sources to give a single picture |
| State | Similar to describe |
| Summarise | Give the major points |

These are only guidelines, the actual wording of your question will determine your approach.

> ➢ **Introduction**

In your introduction refer directly to the title and in order to focus your reader, say how you interpret the title. You can do this by rephrasing the title in your own words

> ➢ **Main body**

In this section you need to present the arguments and evidence for and against the proposed theory. You need to make sure that you evaluate not only the main theory but also mention any competing ideas and why they are not convincing. You need to give the arguments for and against each issue. All of the evidence you present must be referenced to creditable sources.

> ➢ **Conclusion**

Refer back to your question to demonstrate to your reader that you are still answering the set question contained in the title and summarise what you have written about.

> ➢ **Final draft**

Read it aloud to check that it is clearly written. Keep on re-drafting until you are happy with the text. Get somebody independent to read through and look for spelling mistakes and to tell you if it doesn't read well.

Sometimes your tutors will allow you to book an appointment to discuss your first draft of your assignment. It is not a good idea to go and see your tutor the day before it is due to be handed in. Plan your time appropriately to complete your draft.

When you have received feedback you can then start to write up your final copy.

Remember your word count. You will lose marks for being under or over, there is usually a 10% leeway. Make sure you stay within this as some tutors fail your assignment if it is under or over.

## Giving a Presentation

Giving a presentation can be nerve wracking but doesn't need to be. The main thing is that you need to prepare both your content and yourself before you start. Even though you may only be giving a short presentation, be professional about it.

### Preparing yourself:

✓ Dress a little smarter than usual
✓ Check out what equipment will be available in the room
✓ Make handouts for your audience (so they can listen to you)
✓ Breathe deeply to calm yourself
✓ Before you start, think of anything that you are confident at (it doesn't have to have any connection with the presentation it will just give you confident body language)
✓ Stand tall
✓ Look at your audience (tip if you're using a computer or an overhead projector then look at them not the screen behind you)
✓ Don't cross your arms
✓ Don't read from your notes

The following phrase can help any nerves, it puts the presentation into perspective for you. *"No matter what you say, the audience won't remember a word of it in a year's time."*

### Preparing your content:

✓ Use the questions in the following exercise
✓ Keep your visual aids simple and very large font (30 point on Powerpoint). Remember they are not to help you, they are to help the audience understand
✓ Use bullet points
✓ Have no more than 1 slide per minute (and preferably less)
✓ Practise the talk to check the length
✓ Have a clear introduction, middle and if possible end with a summary of the three main points
✓ Use pictures as well as words on your slides
✓ Use any animation functions sparingly - it's about the content
✓ Have a reference list on your final slide

Exercise 14: Questions and checklist for a presentation. Before a presentation use this to help plan. Add a completed one to your portfolio.

| | |
|---|---|
| Title of talk | |
| Date of presentation | |
| Time | |
| Length | |
| Location | |
| Who are the audience? age/gender/background | |
| How many will there be? | |
| What do they know about the topic? | |
| What do they need to know? Why do they need the information? | |
| What don't they need to know? | |
| What questions might they ask? | |
| Can I get the audience to participate? | |
| What equipment is in the room? | |
| How will the room be laid out? (rows/groups) | |
| What audio/visual aids should I use? | |
| Are there any health and safety issues? | |

## Writing a Scientific Lab Report

If you are studying a scientific programme at University then you will carry out some practicals and maybe expected to analyse the results. From this analysis you may, as part of your assessment, have to write a lab report. There should be a set of guidelines provided on how the department wants you to write the report. This will probably be found in the course or module booklet.

The aim of any report is to communicate efficiently and provide sufficient (but not excessive) detail so that others could replicate the study described. It is also for the lecturer to see that you carried out the experiment correctly.

The simple rule for lab reports is that they must be written in the third person, past tense. Never use any names or I, me, we, she, he.

Prepare yourself before you go into the lab by getting all your equipment in one place and reading the method script. Look carefully at the timing and the order of the steps. When you are in the lab, make sure you make a table to put the information in. It is best to get a separate notebook to keep all your results in as bits of paper are easily lost. If you have to make a graph in the lab make it neat and tidy, then you may be able to use it in your report without redrawing it.

The format for a lab report should be:

➤ **Title**
The title should be placed on the head of the report and should be as brief as possible. The title should also reflect the nature of the study, eg. Reaction time as a function of practice. Try to avoid the use of phrases such as 'experiment to show'.

➤ **Abstract**
This should be summarised as briefly as possible in a single paragraph, stating what was done, why and give information about the method and the participants. Tell the reader what was found and state whether the findings were expected or unexpected. You will need to state whether the differences were significant or not (if statistical analysis has been conducted).

➤ **Introduction**

An introduction gives some background about the topic under investigation and includes reference to published work. You must give a reason or reasons for the study, stating which hypothesis is being tested. This should set the scene. It may include a literature review if appropriate.

➤ **Method**

The method should contain a number of subsections.

• **Participants**
  If you have undertaken an experiment where you have taken measurements on people (eg. speed of running in sports or blood pressure in biology) then you need to give relevant details such as age, experience and gender.

• **Research design:**
  **What research methods have you used and why?**
  Describe exactly what happened in the study. Provide sufficient detail and clarity so that a reader unfamiliar with the study could copy it, given the same type of subjects and equipment. Make sure that you rewrite the method in your own words and include any variations you made.

• **Analytical technique:**
  Describe any analytical techniques that you will apply to the data; justifying why they were chosen.

➤ **Results**

The results should give a brief description of the data and then the analysis of it. You should present your analysis as tables and graphs which must have titles and labels.

State what statistical test or equation was applied to the data and report the results of the test. No discussion of the analysis should be written about in this section, this is merely a statement of the main findings of the study.

➤ **Discussion**

You must relate the findings to the hypothesis described in the introduction, and then discuss the findings in relation to previous work. State what further questions are raised by the experiment and what the limitations were.

> **Conclusion**

Summarise your research and state what you would do differently if you were to carry out the experiment again.

> **References**

You need to add a list of any books, articles or internet sites that you have used to help write the report. This should be done using the Harvard referencing system (see later). You may also need to include a literature review.

**The most common things that you should check for are:**

> That the abstract does not contain trivial details which are not of central importance.

> That the findings are summarised, whether statistically significant or not.

> That there is not too much background information in the introduction.

> That there is sufficient rationale for the study.

> That your writing does not include the names of the experimenters or personal pronouns such as I, we, he, she.

---

Exercise 15: Lab report feedback

Add to your portfolio a lab report that you have written for one of your modules. Include the feedback your tutor has provided and reflect on that feedback to say how you would improve on the grade if you were to carry the study out again.

Feedback

........................................................................................................

........................................................................................................

........................................................................................................

........................................................................................................

........................................................................................................

Exercise 16: Reflective Journal

When you finish your degree it will be difficult to remember how you coped with the day to day pressures of being a student. To help you reflect and remember, keep a daily journal of your learning experiences for a month and include it in your portfolio. Look back at the section on reflective thinking to see some questions to help.

Here are a few more questions to consider:

What problems did you encounter?
How did you solve them?
How was your time management?
How was your work/life balance?
What went really well?
Who helped you?
Who did you help?

## Thinking Critically

When you are asked to write about the most important aspects of a theory, issue, argument etc. you will automatically need to think about the arguments for and against. You need to comment on each argument and decide which you agree with and why. This is critical thinking.

Critically doesn't mean make negative comments, it means you should question the information and compare it to other available information.

You need to think of it like being a detective; you need to investigate and check all claims that are being made by everyone involved in the chain of events. This includes your own lecturers and any material you might read. If someone claims a hypothesis is true you need to compare it to the evidence they have provided. Often there may even be conflicting claims based on the same evidence. Who is right, one of them, both or neither? Is the logic sound as they've moved from step to step? It's your job to solve the mystery.

### Analytical Thinking

- ✓ Be objective
- ✓ Examine every aspect of an issue
- ✓ Check the evidence
- ✓ Look for flaws
- ✓ Compare it to other theories
- ✓ Contrast it with other theories
- ✓ Show you understand why people reach certain conclusions
- ✓ Show which arguments and theories you agree with and why (without the use of I)
- ✓ Use the correct academic language

### Critical Questions

- ➤ Who?
- ➤ What?
- ➤ Why?
- ➤ When?
- ➤ Where?
- ➤ How?

# Reading Critically

**When you start to read for your degree you need to start asking questions in your mind - become the detective**

- Is the evidence reliable?

- How reliable is the content of the article?

- Is it from a refereed journal? Have the journal articles that you have chosen been peer reviewed so that they have been read and approved by practitioners and professionals in that field?

- What is the author saying (the abstract and conclusion will give an indication of this)?

- What do you want to get from the article?

- Is there enough detail so that I fully understand this? Or do I need to do more background reading?

- Are there any problems with the methodology that the author has used to gather their evidence?

- Does the evidence provided by the author fully support the arguments put forward or the conclusions drawn?

- How can I use the understanding gained from this article in a wider context (eg. relate it to other aspects of the course/ other modules)?

Always look at the reading materials your lecturers have recommended on the reading lists. These are generally the books or journal articles your tutors want you to use for your assignments. At the end of every lecture the lecturer should provide information on where their reading came from so it is worth making a note of this, as this will give you reading materials for your assessments.

Make sure when using internet sources that they come from reliable sites, otherwise you may lose marks. It is better to use books and journals as the main reading materials for your projects and assignments.
Unless you are giving a short quote (a couple of sentences), correctly referenced, then don't copy the text straight into your work. Always re-word the material as work is often checked out through plagiarism software.

## Writing Critically

New students always tend to start off their writing for their degree by writing descriptively, the more you develop on your degree programme and start to write analytically the more marks you will gain.

Here is an example of the differences:

| Descriptive writing | Critical analysis |
|---|---|
| States what happened | Analyses why something happened and its significance. |
| Describes what something is like | Evaluates strengths and weaknesses of something |
| Explains a theory | Weighs up a theory against others and relates theory to practice |
| States when something works | Investigates why something works or does not work, using examples and case studies |
| Identifies methods used | Explains why methods were used and investigates alternatives. |
| Lists things in order | Uses a logical structure with signposts and links, forms conclusions before moving on, reaches an overall conclusion |

One of the ways to improve your writing is to read as many journal articles as possible on the given subject. Underline or highlight the first three or four words of every paragraph and highlight the key theme throughout the article. From this you will be able to use the beginning of the paragraph for your writing of your assignment and you will be able to use the key themes to back up your critical analysis.

Exercise 17: Thinking critically

Find a research article relating to a recent course you've done.
Identify the key themes that are running through the article.
What arguments are being presented?
What evidence is there to support the arguments?
Does the article reach a conclusion?
Do you think the arguments support the conclusion?

## Referencing

In order for you to complete your assignments you will need to know how to reference correctly. You will lose marks if you do not reference correctly. Referencing is often referred to as citing and means taking ideas or words from something you have read, listened to or watched and putting them into your assignment to support your discussion or analysis. Whenever you use the work of someone else in your coursework, you must reference the source in your assignment text and in your bibliography or reference list.

A reference list is all the references you have referred to in your assignment/project/essay.
A bibliography is a list of all the works that you have read that contributed to your thinking process but that you haven't referenced directly in your writing.
If you reference correctly, your tutors will be able to check your sources for accuracy and you will avoid plagiarism.

Plagiarism means taking somebody's ideas, words or inventions and using them as your own without referencing the source. More commonly now students are cutting and pasting documents from the internet without referencing the source. This means is that when the lecturers submit an electronic copy of your work through plagiarism software it will pick up exactly where the work has come from.

When referencing work, the style that you use in the reference list or bibliography is different from the way that you reference in your text in your assignments. Over the many years that I have been teaching, I always get my first year undergraduate student to complete a simple exercise that will allows them to understand referencing within a text and in a bibliography. Once you have completed this task you will then be able to refer back to the template when you are writing your assignments and gain marks for your referencing style. Here is an example:

**Book single author text:**
In the text you give the author's name and date of the text only e.g. Hepworth (2011)
In your reference list at the end it would look like this:
Hepworth, A., (2011). Studying for your Future. Lancashire. Universe of Learning Ltd.

The best system to use is the Harvard system as your lecturers will understand it and think it to be the professional way to treat references.

## Book references:

An example from the Harvard system for a book, author, (date) published, title, location of publishers, publishers name.

Baker, H., (2010). *Speed Writing Skills Training Course*, Lancashire, Universe of Learning

Then if you referred to the book in the text you'd put (Baker, 2010).

## Journal references

author names, date, article title, journal, volume number, (part number), page number.
This time you'd put the journal name in italics not the article title.

Greenhall, M.H., Lukes, P.J., Petty, M.C. Yarwood, J. and Lvov,Y., 1994. The formation and characterization of Langmuir-Blodgett films of dipalmitoylphosphatidic acid. *Thin Solid Films* 243 (1-2), pp.596-601

## Web references:

In the Harvard system you'd put author, date, page title, web address, date accessed.

Baker, H, (2009), *10 uses for speed writing*, http://www.uolearn.com/speedwriting/10usesofspeedwriting.html, Date accessed 30/06/11

## Exercise 18: Harvard referencing

Find examples of the following types of information sources for your course and write out the references in the Harvard system, saying both how it would look in the text and in the reference section.

| Information | Referencing |
|---|---|
| Book with multiple authors | In text:<br>In reference: |
| Secondary citation | In text:<br>In reference: |
| Contribution in an edited book | In text:<br>In reference: |
| Ebook | In text:<br>In reference: |
| Electronic journal | In text:<br>In reference: |
| Blog | In text:<br>In reference: |
| Official publication or government report | In text:<br>In reference: |

| Information | Referencing |
|---|---|
| Act of parliament | In text:<br>In reference: |
| Thesis | In text:<br>In reference: |
| Newspaper | In text:<br>In reference: |
| Television or radio programme | In text:<br>In reference: |
| Film | In text:<br>In reference: |
| Video/dvd | In text:<br>In reference: |
| Music CD | In text:<br>In reference: |
| Email | In text:<br>In reference: |

Exercise 19: Referencing List

Provide a referencing list for one of your assignments and add a copy to your portfolio. Again, your tutor can look at this to see what aspects you are not getting quite right or to praise you as you have managed to grasp how to reference very early on in your course. Choose a variety of sources such as books, journals, websites to show examples of each type of reference.

Your reference list should be in alphabetical order of the first author's surname. For sources without named authors such as websites they should be listed in alphabetical order of the title.

**Case study: Using referencing**

Once Harvard referencing had been mastered, Sarah found that her assignments looked more professional in their presentation. This helped her to gain more marks as her tutors could see that she had carried out research for the assignment. Sarah used lots of books and journals for her assignments as her tutors emphasised that some websites may not be reliable and that books and journals provided a better resource. Also, the tutors were more familiar with the reading materials Sarah had used. Sarah also realised that it was important that she included a substantial number of resources in the bibliography and referencing list related to the word count of the assignment, for example if her assignments were 3,000 words she used no less than ten references. Sarah says that this is what she feels helped her to achieve her high grades.

## How to carry out a Literature Review

A literature review is an overview of other people's work. The purpose may be to get you to understand the data better, in which case your writing will be descriptive and be a summary of the resources (like a huge abstract covering all the sources). However, the purpose may be for you to combine the sources and synthesis a composite view of all the ideas. Get clarification from your tutor about exactly which type they are expecting. You need to find or research the most relevant comments, materials, studies, reviews, articles and chapters that support your study.

**Types of sources:**

> **Primary source** - this is the actual evidence, examples could be an account from that period in history, a research paper where the authors did the research themselves, a painting from the time of the event, a film, a photo etc.
> **Secondary sources** - where someone is commenting on a primary source or has reviewed range of primary sources.
> **Tertiary source** - where the main content is drawn from other summary documents. So perhaps the author has read only reviews and not used the primary sources themselves.

You need to identify which type of source your tutor is expecting you to use. Do they want you to read books (often tertiary sources) or the sources closer to the real data such as the papers written by people who either carried out the work or have seen the primary sources? To assess how close your chosen resource is to the primary source look at their reference list, if the main references are reviews and books then your author may be quite distant from the original data and be only interpreting other people's work (similar to your own review).

You also need to get a feel for how many sources your tutor wants you to use. It is best to narrow down your research as much as possible; you don't want to read thousands of papers.

You need to largely stick with papers and books not random internet sources. The reason is that books have editors who check the content and papers are refereed by other experts in the area before they are allowed to be published. This doesn't always mean they are correct; just that the reviewers believed that the evidence and arguments presented were logical and fitted with the body of knowledge known up to that point.

81

It can often help to start with someone else's literature review on the same topic. Just put your topic and the word review into your search box. Usually you want to use specialist databases of papers not normal search engines. Ask your librarian for passwords.

## How to carry out a literature review

- ✓ Make an action plan to make sure you have enough time for each part
- ✓ Write out a summary statement of up to 3 sentences of what the review will be about
- ✓ Ask staff for their expertise in recommending reading materials
- ✓ Look at your recommended reading on your programme booklet
- ✓ Find out who the key researchers are in your area of research and read around other work they may have done
- ✓ Do computer searches, as an academic you need to try and avoid sites that are not reliable
- ✓ Read, read, read and record: full references, hypothesis, subjects, methodology, statistics, findings, future studies/research, limitations of the study, any other key references
- ✓ Group similar references together
- ✓ Look for key themes emerging
- ✓ If your references agree then the synthesis is easier
- ✓ If you find conflicting arguments you may need to look for later review articles which help to understand the differing points of view.
- ✓ Once you've read all your material make a plan for writing, a mindmap, concept map or flow chart are great ways of getting an overview
- ✓ Always stay focused, keep your research question in mind

## Reading your sources

- ➢ Collect your sources
- ➢ Write down around three questions you need to answer
- ➢ Look at every page for two seconds
- ➢ Evaluate the references (How useful will they be and how easy to read?)
- ➢ Prioritise them in order of importance
- ➢ Leave it one for two days (this lets your mind organise the data)
- ➢ For each reading source read the abstract or a short summary, then again look at each page for two seconds . Then read in the order that makes most sense to you. You don't need to read everything.

For more advice on reading get a book on speed reading like Speed reading Training Course, ISBN 9781849370219, Greenhall (2011).

It may be a good idea to buy some file cards and note down the name of the book, year, author, publisher, place of publishing and quotes you could use. On the other side, write a summary of the source.

If you keep all your file cards in a record box you will always have a record for your bibliography. There is software that helps you to track your references, two common ones are Refworks and Endnote. Ask your librarian whether your university has installed any referencing software and you can store all your assignment references in one place. Alternatively you could use excel or any other spreadsheet/database programme to store the data.

University libraries subscribe to most journals electronically now and you can access them for free, just ask for a password at the library. If you find a book, that your library doesn't stock, you can request it via interlibrary loan. Interlibrary loans can take a while to arrive and there may be a charge.

## Writing the review

➢ Look at the section on essay writing and critical writing again
➢ Have an introduction explaining why the review is being done and what sort of sources you've used, explain the structure of your review
➢ The main part should have some logical order, this depends on the content of your review but some options are:
   • By chronological order of the information
   • By chronological order of the sources
   • By trend, a section for each new idea and links as to how they led into each other
   • By research group (particularly for scientific reviews)
   • By major ideas or themes
   • By geographical location
➢ The summary should bring together the arguments and perhaps include questions to consider that arise from the material (particularly if the purpose is to start a dissertation or research project)

> Exercise 20: Literature Review
>
> Include a copy of a literature review in your file that you have prepared for one of your assignments.

## Preparing for your Exams

Once you know the dates for your examinations it will take some planning to get yourself ready for the date. Many students make the common mistake of leaving everything to the last minute.

- ✓ The first thing that you need to do is to organise your notes to find out what you do know and what you don't

- ✓ Reduce your notes to key headings, points and references

- ✓ Produce a mindmap of all you have to revise

- ✓ Print off lecture notes from either student folders, your virtual learning environment or files that the university have provided for you

- ✓ Print off past papers, sometimes there is still work left on the system from the year before so you can access last years examination questions to help you revise for this year's subjects

### Passing an exam starts in your lectures and seminars:

At the end of lecture notes or during lectures there will be task questions. These might give some indication of what will be on your examination paper.

Make sure you understand how many marks will be required for you to pass your exam. It is also important for you to understand the marking of each question, for instance if there is a question that is worth 6 marks, make sure you write down six points or three lots of in depth answers so that you will be awarded two marks for each relevant point.

It is really important to attend all of your lectures, it is well researched that the students who turn up for lectures obtain the greatest marks. You can't understand all the relevant points made in a lecture from a Powerpoint presentation, you have to engage in discussion and listen in the lecture to the questions that are being asked.

Often in your lectures at exam time your lecturers will direct you indiscreetly to areas of importance for revision. Always remember it is in the key interest of a lecturer to teach you to pass your exams, not to have to fail you.

When looking at formulas in lectures and seminars, remember them for your exams, as these will not usually be written down for you.

Work out the answers to a range of possible exam questions for each topic, so that you feel able to deal with almost any question that might be set in the topics you have chosen.

Draw up a timetable for your exams, which will require you to work out exactly how much time you have to revise. Don't leave it to the last minute. At least four weeks before your exam begin to put together your revision notes. The pitfalls of revision include leaving revision to the last minute and finding ways of putting off revision (such as urgent things that need to be done i.e. watching television and socialising).

## Making revision notes

Some people think that just by working hard and repetition that the material will stick so they follow strategies like:

- ✗ Reading through notes over and over again
- ✗ Writing notes out over and over again
- ✗ Writing out essays and learning them off by heart

These can help but it is much better to engage in actively reorganising the data.

- ✓ Condense your notes or mindmap them
- ✓ Use colour for different concepts
- ✓ Make flash cards of the key points
- ✓ Read your notes out aloud
- ✓ Meet with someone else and discuss likely exam questions
- ✓ Practise previous exam questions

It may also be a good idea when you are reading your journal and books for revision, as well as writing assignments for exams, to make a note on file cards of the title of the book, the year the book was written, the place the book was published and the publisher's name. On the opposite side of the card you can note down key themes and quotes that you want to use from the book. This way the book can go back to the library and you have a copy of everything you require from that resource.

Another good way to organise your notes is to colour code your notes either into subjects or a traffic light system whereby you use green, red and yellow to distinguish what you have read, what you need to read and what you can put to one side to read over again and again. This will help to keep you organised and keep your notes distinguished.

## Memory

You will need to use your memory effectively when you are revising and one way to do this is to read your notes after the lecture, a day after the lecture and a week after the lecture. Once you come to revise for your exams you will be able to read over the notes again and then put them into the coloured category that means you understand and memorise what has been written on that certain part of the subject. This timing has been scientifically proved to be the best way to memorise complex facts.

In your working memory you only have space for 7 items at once so when you're revising it its best to stick to just 4 ideas at once. That way you have space to make the connections to the rest of the information stored in your brain.

If you revise in bursts of 15 minutes, with a short 2 minute break, it helps to refocus your attention as most people's attention span is about 20 minutes.

Always give yourself a comfort break after one or two hours. Go and do something else, get bit of fresh air and drink a glass of water as this will help to rehydrate your brain.

**What you need to take with you to your exam**

- ❏ Pens (2 black/blue and 1 red, [if allowed])
- ❏ Eraser
- ❏ Pencil
- ❏ Sharpener
- ❏ Highlighter pen
- ❏ Ruler
- ❏ Calculator
- ❏ Any open book materials that you are allowed
- ❏ Bottle of Water

**During the exam**

- ✓ Start by reading the instructions, the format of the exam may have changed even if it has been the same for 10 years
- ✓ Read all the questions carefully and allocate the time you have for each, allowing checking time at the end
- ✓ Choose which ones to attempt - it is usually best to start with the easiest as then you'll gain confidence and get in the flow
- ✓ Take your time when selecting the correct answer during multiple choice exams
- ✓ As soon as you get in write down formulas and details that you have remembered
- ✓ Read over your answers again at the end

---

Exercise 21: Exam preparation/final project preparation.

Draw up a revision timetable using your time management grid (exercise 8) to show where you will be able to fit in time for revision.

## Degree Enrichment

It is really important that you utilise the time that you have away from the university, spending quality time progressing towards your chosen goals and dreams. This is so that an employer can look at your curriculum vitae and see that you have done work above and beyond what was expected of you at university.

**Degree enrichment may involve the following:**

➢ Volunteering to help out in a school

➢ Volunteering / working in a care home

➢ Working for an organisation or charity fund raising

➢ Coaching a sport abroad

➢ Organising events for children during the school holidays.

➢ Working in summer holiday camps where students are paid for working with young adults and children, particularly in America.

➢ Working with Voluntary Services Overseas, which is an organisation that can give you the opportunity to work in third world countries making the lives of the poor people better using the skills that you have.

➢ Going into schools and listening to the children read.

➢ Contacting the local parish council to see if there are any schemes you can become involved in.

➢ Volunteering to be a Samaritan.

➢ Sports teams

➢ Positions of responsibility in your clubs and college

➢ Part time work

➢ Etc.

**Case study: Volunteering**

Jenny had already completed a first aid course as part of her work with the St. John Ambulance. She had worked at events before she came to University. Through her course she then completed a further first aid certificate. She offered her services as a first aider to the student union during their sports activities. This often meant travelling away with the teams to other universities.

Jenny was offered the opportunity to apply for a position working for the Red Cross, even though this was nothing to do with her degree programme. This set Jenny up with a graduate job, earning a good salary with the opportunity of travelling around the world to different countries, training with the British Red Cross.

Exercise 22: Reflection of your first year programme.

State what you have enjoyed the most about your first year on your degree programme.

What do you feel you have learned on this year's programme?

Are you happy with the grades that you have been achieving for your assignments and projects?

What do you need to do next year to improve your grades for your degree programme?

If you had to go through the first year again, is there anything you would change or do differently?

**Notes:**

**Notes:**

# Chapter 3
# Year 2, Skills Development

"The people who get on in this world are the people who get up and look for the circumstances they want, and, if they can't find them, make them." George Bernard Shaw

# Chapter 3:
# Year 2, Skills Development

During your first year of University you have hopefully settled in, enjoyed the social aspect of university life and you've received your end of year results. These results either give you the wake up call you need or you may decide that you are doing really well and need to keep up the standard to achieve a high degree classification.

Normally, it is at Christmas time of the second year when students start to realise that if they pulled their socks up and took their studies a little more seriously that they could achieve a really high grade for their degree programme. As well as working towards your degree, you have to start also thinking 'outside the box' about employment, as it is during this year that you are laying the foundations for future employability.

The next sections will guide you through exactly what you need to be doing to prepare yourself for employment.

Once you have started the second year of your study, it is really important to keep focusing on your goals and also to spend some time thinking about career prospects. Have a look now at the goals and dreams you set last year and see how you're getting on. Do you have any new goals to add?

When you first started out doing your degree, you may have had a career in mind and then after the first year of study you may have changed your mind about your future. It may even change again when you go into your third year. It is also quite common in your third year to still not know what career you want to follow. This section will help you to gain the skills required to be able to say to an employer, 'I have this skill and this is how I have applied it' and also to help guide you onto the right path of your chosen career.

**Reflection for Year 2.**

At the end of your first year you reflected back on what went really well for you during the year. When you carry out an assessment grid for your 2nd year, reflect upon what you need to do to stay focused and achieve really good grades.

Remember this year's grades go towards your degree classification.

Exercise 23: Action Planning

By considering these issues it will make you become more focused on what you need to do.

What do you have to do to improve the way that you carried out research for your assignments?

........................................................................................

........................................................................................

........................................................................................

........................................................................................

........................................................................................

........................................................................................

........................................................................................

Would you change anything about the processes that you used last year eg. time management, preparation, presentation, peers you mix with at university, tutor support, learning support, etc.?

........................................................................................

........................................................................................

........................................................................................

........................................................................................

........................................................................................

........................................................................................

........................................................................................

Exercise 24: For each module in your year complete a module assessment grid (see exercise 11). Then make estimates of your grades.

| Module number and title | Estimated grade | Actual grade |
| --- | --- | --- |
| | | |
| | | |
| | | |
| | | |
| | | |
| | | |
| | | |
| | | |

Exercise 25: Complete an action plan and assessment grid to reflect on what you need to do to become more effective in your second year.

You may want to list all your assignments that are due to be completed and what you must do in order to reach the deadlines.

| Action required | Date for completion | Actual date completed |
| --- | --- | --- |
| | | |
| | | |
| | | |
| | | |
| | | |
| | | |
| | | |

97

## Strengths Weaknesses Experiences Achievements Threats (SWEAT)

You may be asked at interview to carry out a SWEAT or SWOT analysis. The O is Opportunities that may be ahead of you.

➤ **Strengths**

Write a paragraph about what you are really good at doing. What do you feel confident about? For example are you confident at speaking to large groups of students, good at presentation skills or proficient at organising meetings and large events. Five strengths would be sufficient.

➤ **Weaknesses**

Write a paragraph about what you feel lets you down about yourself from a personal perspective as well as from an academic perspective. This may include those skills that you are not good at that you need to improve upon. For example, not finishing things, poor time management, writing skills etc. Three of these will be sufficient.

➤ **Experiences**

Write a paragraph about the good experiences that have happened to you that have helped you to develop your skills. This may be experiences you might have gained whilst studying for your degree or other activities. For example passing your driving test, working in a team, a personal challenge such as a sponsored walk etc.

➤ **Achievements**

Write a paragraph about your achievements in the past twelve months. This can be through your work or maybe through a hobby. It could include becoming good at something, competing in a sporting event etc. We are often poor at celebrating our successes so dig deep and what you think isn't an achievement may be a huge achievement to someone else so write it down.

➤ **Threats**

Write a paragraph about what takes you out of your comfort zone. What do you feel is more challenging to you that you will have to work on? What makes you feel very uncomfortable before the event occurs, during the event or after the event? What could stop you achieving your goals: illness, other people, lack of resources, etc.?

Exercise 26: Carry out a SWEAT analysis for your coming year.

**Strengths:**

**Weaknesses:**

**Experiences:**

**Achievements:**

**Threats:**

## Critical Analysis

In your first year of your degree programme you are asked to write quite descriptively using research that you have read about to back up what you are describing. Now in the second year of your programme it is important that you increase your academic ability and learn to write at a higher level.

To enable you to write at this higher level you will be encouraged to read more books, journals etc. so that you can build up the resources you need to complete your assignments. Whilst you are reading through the materials you have chosen it is important to keep an open mind on the key themes and arguments that are being presented. We need to form an opinion as to which articles are supporting one side of the argument and find other articles that are going against the other's theories. Critical analysis is about presenting those findings, putting over the different points of view and writing in the third person (unless otherwise stated) that these are the conclusions that have been summarised.

If you look carefully at your assessment criteria that you get with your assignment brief, you will be able to see that often you need to master the skill of critical analysis to get the highest marks.
Examples of assessment criteria could be:

### Analysis and Interpretation

**70% 1st** Comprehensive coverage, focus and progression of the theoretical aspects. Precise and coherent evaluation of current guidelines of the uses of....

**(60-69%) 2:1** Appropriate coverage of the theoretical aspects, good progression and focus. Largely appropriate evaluation of current guidelines.

**(50-59%) 2:2** Reasonable coverage of the theoretical aspects and some appropriate focus and progression. Reasonable outline of evaluation of current guidelines but not fully explained.

**(40-49%) 3rd** Some coverage of the theoretical aspects but with little progression of focus. Basic evaluation of current guidelines that lacked clarity and were not fully explained.

**<39% Fail** Little coverage of the theoretical aspects illustrating little disciplinary knowledge. Largely inappropriate outline of evaluation of guidelines

Exercise 27: Critical analysis

Write about an issue on your degree programme, this can be about any subject. Write about aspects of your chosen issue.

Use evidence to back up your arguments for or against.
Use examples to back up your argument
Reach a conclusion.

## Problem Solving

With any task that you have to carry out whether it be in your personal or professional working life there maybe problems to solve. Some people bury their heads in the sand, wishing that the problem would go away and others tackle it head on like a bull in a china shop, when they could have spent some time evaluating their outcomes.

Worrying about a problem is a waste of good energy, you might as well use that energy to get the problem solved.

Let's look at a strategy for problem solving.

Firstly analyse your to do list for the day and identify if the problem is one of your priorities for the day. It might mean that if you solve this problem now or today it frees your mind up to deal with other issues.

*"Don't put off till tomorrow what you can do today."*

Sometimes when we have a lot to deal, with particularly when you are in a leadership or team situation, problems will build up until we feel that we can't deal with any of them and you may become overwhelmed. This can lead to breakdowns in communication, confusion over what task to do next and possibly even illness.

Exercise 28: Problem Solving Reflection

Write a reflective piece of writing about an incident or experience where you had to use problem solving skills to enable the incident or experience to have a positive outcome. If the experience that you are writing about didn't have a positive outcome state why and write about what you may do next time in that situation on reflection to change the situation from a negative to a positive outcome.

You may need to discuss your problem with somebody neutral to the situation. Ask them to listen to your point of view and add to your solution rather than criticise it.

Also, consider at this point what would happen if you didn't achieve the desired outcome. Would it be detrimental to your own health and well being?

Exercise 29: Problem solving

Identify a problem and write it down as a question.

...........................................................................................

...........................................................................................

Write a list of who it involves.

...........................................................................................

...........................................................................................

Write down the outcome you want to achieve from solving the problem.

...........................................................................................

...........................................................................................

...........................................................................................

Write a step by step list on how to tackle the problem.

...........................................................................................

...........................................................................................

...........................................................................................

...........................................................................................

...........................................................................................

...........................................................................................

Will you have to look at other alternatives or maybe a compromise?

...........................................................................................

For lots more problem solving questions see a list developed by the CIA http://bbh-labs.com/how-the-cia-define-problems-plan-solutions-the-phoenix-checklist

## Motivating Others

In order to get through our everyday life we have to learn to have respect for others and how to get along with other people using different types of behaviour patterns. We all soon learn what is acceptable behaviour and what is not.

As part of your learning programme you will be grouped with peers. Some you will see as having acceptable behaviour and some not. Yet, it will be out of your control to walk away. This may be because you may have a group presentation to put together or are working on a project where you've been assigned to groups.

Some people are born leaders in situations like this and some people will just sit back and let others do all the work.

The most common complaint of group work is that certain individuals have completed all the work and then others who hardly participated still gained a good mark as it was awarded to the group as a whole.

In order for individuals to be able to work together successfully the group has to become motivated.

Motivation levels will differ across the time of the planning of the presentation/projects depending on what other issues people have going on in their lives.

To keep others motivated it is important to have clear goals and a clear aim at the beginning of the procedure, to share the work load out equally and give everybody a time scale. If one leader cannot be agreed, have two for different parts of the project and instead of having a leader over the whole project have a coordinator who manages the two leaders. This way everybody gets to take part equally, fairly and satisfactorily.

Exercise 30: Motivating others

At interview for a job you may be asked how you have actively motivated others.

Think about an event where you have had to motivate someone or a group of people to do something.

Think about the process, how did you achieve the desired outcome?

What skills did you use?

## Effective Team Working

A team is composed of a number of individuals working towards a common goal. You may enjoy working on your own, working at your own pace, not being told by anyone what to do and organising your work the way that you want it to be carried out. However, sometimes we work with other people to complete a task. A good exercise to have a look at is 'Belbin Team Roles', this will establish what role you usually play within a team, www.belbin.com. You may identify yourself as being the plant, the monitor evaluator, coordinator, resource investigator, implementer, completer finisher, team worker, shaper or specialist. A good team needs a mixture of these personalities and none are better than the others.

It is a really good idea to know how you operate in a team situation. One of the most important skills to make your team work effectively is communication.

### Here are some ideas for effective team managers:

❑ Respect all of your team members.

❑ Make sure the team understands what is being asked of them.

❑ Make sure they know the project requirement thoroughly and know the project target is achievable and by when.

❑ Each member needs to have clearly defined roles and responsibilities to avoid confusion or overwork.

❑ Let everyone have their say.

❑ Listen to other people's opinions and use their suggestions but explain that if it doesn't work you'll try another way.

❑ Ask for feedback and suggestions.

❑ Give reasons for your actions.

❑ Praise your team.

❑ Avoid blaming others when work is not completed. Find out why it has not been completed and draw up a different strategy.

❑ Find out if one of the team members is facing any problems completing the work on time, find out the root cause and address the issue.

❑ Communication and approachability are very important.

Did you tick all the boxes? Then your team will have an excellent chance of working effectively.

As an effective team worker you may have to guide and support other team members and learn to understand the different behaviours and personalities and qualities that all team members bring to the group. Always stay focused on the goal and what ways the team can work best to achieve that goal.

Exercise 31: Effective team work

Questions may be asked about team work during job interviews so you need to have examples ready. Think about a situation where you have been part of a team.
What role did you play within the team?
Were you happy with your performance within that team?
How did the team stay motivated to carry out tasks together?
Did you have any problems carrying out your roles and if so how did you solve the problems that occurred?

## Leadership Skills

Beyond the personal traits of a leader there are specific skills people must learn to master if they want to become a leader.

You must be an effective communicator to enable you to motivate people to work toward the group goal. You need excellent negotiation skills to help make sure everyone contributes their best to the project. You must be a good planner to be able to devise a plan to achieve the goal and then encourage people to complete the goal. Leaders must be realistic, polite but insistent, they constantly and consistently drive forward their goal.

*"No goal is achievable unless you chip away at it every day." Ackah.*

### Do you regard yourself to be a good leader yes/no?

If not, what do you feel you need to improve to enable you to take on the leadership role?

➢ Believe in yourself more to increase your confidence?
➢ Greater clarity of your goals?
➢ Have a better knowledge of the skills and personalities of your group?

If you do regard yourself to be a good leader:

➢ What three words would you use to describe your leadership qualities?

Again in an interview situation you may be asked to talk about or demonstrate how you have used your leadership qualities, providing examples.

Exercise 32: Leadership skills.

What opportunities have you had to practise your leadership skills?

Can you plan any activities in the near future to give yourself more leadership skills?

Are there any leaders you admire?

How do they lead?

What do you think a good manager/leader needs to be able to do?

Can you find any books, particularly biographies of great leaders?

**Case study: Working alongside your course**

Julia attended university for three years and graduated with a 2:1 degree. She took an access course to get to university as she did not have the traditional entry requirements to enrol on her course.

Throughout her course there were opportunities to complete a work placement and work shadow health professionals as well as to take part time employed work at the weekends. Julia completed this whilst going through a break up of her marriage, losing her house and having nowhere to live with her family. She then worked as a volunteer for a company for six months, three hours per week offering her services in all the areas that the company provided.

Through this Julia was offered an excellent full time post with a starting salary upon graduating at £26,000. Julia was delighted with this and she said

*"You only get out of it, what you put in."*

Julia has now started a part time master's degree and is working towards a PhD so that she can get an even better job as her boys get older and less dependent upon her.

Exercise 33: What other skills do you have that will help you with your work?

We've talked about some skills that are useful in work and in study, what other skills do you have that an employer might be interested in?

......................................................................................................................
......................................................................................................................
......................................................................................................................
......................................................................................................................
......................................................................................................................

**Notes:**

**Notes:**

# Chapter 4
# Years 2 and 3,
# Preparing for Work

"Often people attempt to live their lives backwards: they try to have more things, or more money, in order to do more of what they want so that they will be happier. The way it actually works is the reverse. You must first be who you really are, then, do what you need to do, in order to have what you want." Margaret Young

# Chapter 4:
# Years 2 and 3,
# Preparing for Work

## Volunteering

Sometimes in life we have to be prepared to go the extra mile to get to where we want to be.

Through your goal setting one of the aims may be to gain experience in your chosen field. If there is no paid work available in those areas you may want to give up a couple of hours of your time every week or once a month to work shadow or volunteer.

There is statistical evidence to prove that employment positions are given to someone who is already doing the job.

You can volunteer for a few hours to demonstrate your enthusiasm. Once your foot is in the door you will be able to see what opportunities are available. The amount of time you're able to get with a company maybe very small but it will be a great asset when you come to apply for other jobs and you will have specific examples you can use. There are specific websites you can log onto for volunteering opportunities.

www.do-it.org.uk is a very popular website that has a database of voluntary and charitable opportunities. There are lots of voluntary organisations which you can apply for, some volunteering opportunities are available overseas, but you do have to pay. It may be useful to contact your local place of worship to find out if they have any projects you could help out with abroad. The National Trust offers a lot of positions too.

It looks really impressive on your CV if you have been a volunteer at some point, even if it is just for a few events.

## Exercise 34: Volunteering

Make a list of volunteering opportunities you might like to become involved in. It may be towards your chosen career or it may be something that you aspire to carrying out eg. helping to build a school in Ghana.

Write a paragraph on each of the volunteering schemes that you have been involved with and say how you feel they benefitted you.

## Career Searches

It may be a good idea to book an appointment with your careers advisor whilst you are at university as it is a free service. Some universities extend their service for one year after you have left the institution to help you to start along your career path. Some students still don't know what they want to do in their second year. Some students think they know right from the start what they want to do and as they progress on their degree they change their minds. Some final year students still don't know what they want to do at the end of their course, so it can all get to be quite confusing. Visit your careers department early on as they have lots of great resources.

Through the use of goal setting you can devise a plan of where you see yourself and potential earnings. Often students say to me "I really don't know what I would like to do when I leave university." I've developed a series of questions to help them think about the type of environment and roles they see for themselves. Have a go, you can choose more than one option!

---

### Exercise 35: What do you want your work life to be like?

1. What environment do you see yourself working in?

| | |
|---|---|
| ❏ Indoors | ❏ Self employed |
| ❏ Outdoors | ❏ Public sector |
| ❏ Office environment | ❏ Big corporate |
| ❏ Factory | ❏ Small company |
| ❏ Field | ❏ Charity |
| ❏ Lab | ❏ Travelling around locally |
| ❏ Forest | ❏ Travelling nationally |
| ❏ Beach | ❏ Travelling the world |
| ❏ Hospital | ❏ Confined to one place |
| ❏ School | ❏ At a desk |
| ❏ University | ❏ Doing a physical job |

Other .................................................................................................

---

2. When in the day do you want to work?

- ❑ Daytime only
- ❑ Days and evenings
- ❑ Nights
- ❑ Shift work - mixed times
- ❑ Weekends
- ❑ Don't mind

3. What type of people do you want to work with?

- ❑ Children
- ❑ Young adults
- ❑ Prefer to work alone
- ❑ Adults only
- ❑ Elderly
- ❑ Mixed
- ❑ Special needs
- ❑ Don't mind

4. What interests you?

........................................................................................................

........................................................................................................

........................................................................................................

........................................................................................................

........................................................................................................

5. What salary do you want to be potentially earning in 5 years time?

........................................................................................................

6. What salary do you potentially want to be earning in 10 years time?

........................................................................................................

7. How many years do you want to stay in your job?

........................................................................................................

8. Where do you see yourself in 10 years time? This could involve a house, family, moving abroad moving into a managerial role etc. Where would you like to be living and what sort of house?

....................................................................

....................................................................

....................................................................

....................................................................

....................................................................

....................................................................

9. What salary is your absolute minimum you can work for to allow you to live and possibly pay back your student loan.

....................................................................

10. What salary do you want to be earning to live a comfortable lifestyle?

....................................................................

After answering those ten questions we can start to get an idea of the areas you would like to work in and from this you can establish whether you will need further training or are there already the jobs out there to match your skills.

Following is a list of job websites you can start to have a look at. Step out of your comfort zone as there is a big world out there and you may want to consider working abroad for a short time which could possibly end up long term or via a promotion back to this country.

List of websites to look for jobs

www.jobsite.co.uk (job centres)   www.jobs.ac.uk (universities)
www.hays.co.uk   www.whatjobsite.com/
www.totaljobs.com   jobs.guardian.co.uk
www.monster.co,uk   www.executiveheadhunters.co.uk
www.jobrapido.co.uk   www.office-angels.com
www.fish4.co.uk/jobs   www.pertemps.co.uk
www.reed.co.uk

There will be specific jobsites for subjects that you are interested in. eg. sport related websites, jobs specific to nursing etc. The best place to find jobs is in the specialist magazines for your chosen area, eg. New Scientist, Times Educational Supplement.

You should start in your second year to look for graduate positions. Many applications have to be in around Christmas time in your final year so you don't have much time when you return after the summer.

## Exercise 36: Career search

Complete three jobs searches for the areas you are interested in working in. Download the job descriptions and highlight the key skills and attributes the employer is looking for. State how you already match those skills, or what you need to go and do to acquire more experience. eg. this might involve some work shadowing, or volunteer work.

Find someone who already does the job and ring or email them and ask if they have 10 mins to tell you about the job (the worst they could do is put the phone down or delete your email!).

## Researching Possible Employers

It is vital to find out as much as possible about possible employers. This is to help you decide who you'd like to work for and also to help you when you do get an interview.

To start identifying potential employers you first need to think about your future lifestyle. What you need to establish whilst you are doing your degree is how flexible you are about travelling to work and where will you be living? Will you be going back to your home town on completion of your degree? Do you want to travel with your work? Would you like to work in another country?

Use all your vacations to gain as much experience in your chosen field, work experience, work shadowing or volunteering to go and work inside a company. You may have to work for free; this again shows willingness and shows the employer you are worth employing. Make a list of all your ideal employers where you would like to see yourself working, and then focus in on a few to investigate further.

---

Exercise 37: Researching potential employers.

Make a database (spreadsheet programmes like excel can be used) of names, addresses, websites and any information you find out in your research of companies or institutions you would like to work for.

Your tutors may be able to help you with this, or your university careers centre. The careers centre should have access to graduate directories.

Then do some research about each company. Find out:

➤ What does the company do?
➤ Look at their recent annual report to check how well they are doing.
➤ Where are they based?
➤ What is the structure of the company (what departments are there)?
➤ What is the history of the company or institution?
➤ What types of jobs might be available for future promotion?
➤ Who is the managing director and what is their background?
➤ How many graduates might they take on each year?
➤ Do they have a graduate training programme?
➤ Does it feel like you'd fit in?

## Curriculum Vitae (CV)

The world of work is very competitive and you need to make sure your CV sells you. Interviewers can have hundreds of applications so you need to make your CV easy to read, as short as possible and professional looking. As a guideline your CV should be no longer than 2 pages. Make sure at least two other people proofread it for you, preferably someone who has experience of job selection or staff in the careers department. A good tip is to use a table to lay out the information but have the grid lines hidden, that way it is easy to line up everything. Use bold and larger fonts for emphasis, not underlining as it is seen as old fashioned. Do remember as well you may get googled so check out your online presence and perhaps even consider having a blog or website with further information about yourself.

### Example of the contents of a good CV

### Name

### Address

### Tel no.                 Email address

### Personal Profile

This is a statement that describes your qualities in about six lines only for example:-

A hard working, totally trustworthy business/ sport media/ nursing graduate with the ability to work as part of a team or independently. Extensive experience working with children within a sport/media/ hospital setting. Flexible, confident and determined to achieve desired goals and outcomes.

### Education

Name of University        Degree and grade
Other significant subjects you have studied on your degree programme.
Name of School/College
Subjects studied to A'level with grades.
Subjects studied to GCSE with grades (always list maths and English first)

## Work History

Name of Company month/ year to month/ year. You usually put these in order of most recent first going to the most distant but if you have had a significant role that will impress the interviewer put it near the top of the list.

## Achievements

Write down anything that you are proud of, for example:

First team rugby captain
Travelled extensively around Europe and Asia.
Worked in New Zealand
Represented the school in overseas exchange programme.

## Key Skills

Analysis, research, problem solving, time management etc. State how you have achieved these skills through your degree programme, perhaps give specific examples.

## IT

State the different information technology programmes that you have become proficient in using at university. These might include word, excel, SPSS for statistics, data bases, web design etc.

## Interpersonal skills

State how you have either stayed motivated or motivated others on your course. State how you have developed your skills to become a team player. Have you got examples of your leadership skills, sales or negotiating skills?

## Interests

List all your hobbies and activities you are interested in.

## Referees

Do not put references on request. Usually giving two referees is sufficient. Ask permission before giving a referee's details.

| | |
|---|---|
| Name | Name |
| Position | Position |
| Address | Address |
| Postcode | Postcode |
| Tel no. | Tel no. |
| email address | email address. |

It is a really good idea to invest in some good quality cream paper to print your CV onto as it makes your CV stand out from all the rest when you apply for a post.

Make sure you really sell yourself on your CV, especially your skills as this is what employers are interested in. You should have a standard version but be prepared to add extra bits or change the order to fit the needs of the employer.

---

**Exercise 38: Curriculum Vitae**

Using the template above to create an up-to-date CV that you could send to an employer.

---

**Notes:**

**Case Study: Being realistic**

Michael is a semi-professional football player for local team, potential earnings £700 per week. He's now in the third year of university.

Michael is realistic and knows that he will not make a professional football player, even though this was his childhood dream. He has long term injury problems with his knee and this stops him progressing any further. Michael does not want to move too far away, on completion of his degree, as he would still like to play for his team. Now as Michael is in his final year at university he has to realistically consider his future. Michael has started to apply for local graduate positions. He has been to the careers department at his university to obtain a copy of the graduate directories that are available free of charge to students. These directories advertise all the graduate positions all around the country.

Michael has updated his CV and has a standard covering letter ready to send out to employers.

He has had these documents checked by his personal tutor and Michael is now concentrating on achieving good grades for the modules he is studying so that he can achieve the 2:1 degree classification. This is also required for the positions he would like to apply for. Michael in the meantime is also attending a primary school one morning a week listening to children read and work shadowing primary school teachers as this will keep Michael's further options open for the future if he would like to pursue a career in teaching.

**Notes:**

# Chapter 5
# The Final Year

"There will come a time when you believe everything is finished. That will be the beginning." Louis L'Amour

# Chapter 5:
# The Final Year

When you enter your final year of study, reflection will play a large part in your undergraduate and postgraduate degree process. You are now preparing to leave the University to enter employment or to go onto studying a higher degree. You may have decided at the start of your course to work in a specific field and by now have a totally different perspective on what you want to do.

Make sure you keep up with the good habits you've developed in time management. Keep using your weekly planner and the module assessment forms. This year you'll have some large pieces of work that test a wide range of skills.

---

Exercise 39: Revisiting your dreams and goals

Find your dreams and goals sheets from year 1.
Which ones have you accomplished?
Which ones would you change?
What else have you achieved that you are proud of?
Download and fill in a new goals sheet from www.uolearn.com and add it to your file.

---

Exercise 40: Reflection of your degree programme so far

At the beginning of your final year, write a reflective piece of writing covering:

What degree classification you are heading for?

What do you need to do this year to achieve the best degree you can?

On reflection from last year, what worked well for you on your degree programme and what didn't?

What do you recognise that you have to improve in order for you to achieve higher grades?

Exercise 41: Action planning and assessment grid

What do you have to do to improve the way that you carry out research for your assignments?
Would you change anything about the processes that you used eg. time management, preparation, presentation, peers you mix with at university, tutor support, learning support? By considering these issues it will make you become more focused on what you need to do.
Complete an action plan to reflect on what you must do to become more effective in the final year of your degree programme.

You may want to list all your assignments that are due to be completed and what you must do in order to reach the deadlines.

See exercises 24 and 25 for tables to help with this

## Time management - juggling everything

Each year of your course you should complete the weekly planner in exercise 8. However, as life is getting more complicated you need to be more ruthless with your time and start to say no to things that are not high priorities.

One method of looking at your priorities is to use the urgent/ important gird. You make a list of everything you do and then put them into one of four categories.

> ### Urgent and important
These are things with immediate deadlines that if they don't get done will have a negative impact on your life. If too many of your activities fall in this area you will be lurching from crisis to crisis. You need to use goal and action planning to move the activities into the next quadrant.

> ### Not urgent but important
This is where most of your time should be spent. The important things that are going to take forward your dreams and goals but that don't have to be done in a panic. The trouble is things from the other three areas always seem to take priority if you don't plan your time properly. Particularly the tasks in the next category.

> ### Urgent but not important
These are things that demand your immediate attention but are not important to you. Many of these can be caused by your colleagues' poor time management. Friends demanding you help them with a task they have and they need it done right now. If this is happening frequently you need to start setting boundaries on your time.

> ### Not urgent nor important
Hmm, if you're spending a lot of time doing these sort of things you are probably procrastinating on a bigger task in the not urgent but important area and this will eventually lead to pushing that activity into the urgent and important and causing another crisis. This is definitely the area you need to look at using the word NO.

### Exercise 42: Prioritising your work

Make a list of everything you do over a period of 2 weeks. Then categorise them into this grid. Then assess how you prioritise your time between the four areas and write an action plan for improving the way you work.

|  | URGENT | NOT-URGENT |
|---|---|---|
| IMPORTANT |  |  |
| NOT IMPORTANT |  |  |

## Presenting Your Research

As part of a degree course you may be asked to do a dissertation or project report. Often a dissertation will be a key piece of research that you will be asked to write of around 8,000-15,000 words.

When you are choosing your dissertation or project, have a look to see what literature has been written on this topic already. You may want to turn your research into a paper, poster or a presentation at a conference. There are lots of student conferences around the country and worldwide where students are given the chance to voice and present their research ideas and findings. Try and find a piece of research which is unique that hasn't been researched lots of times. The best people to ask are your mentors, personal tutors or head of year.

Also, remember you are going to be spend a lot of time working on this piece of research, so it is important that you find a subject you are interested in, otherwise you may lose interest part way through and not be motivated enough to strive for a high grade.

Before you decide on your proposal for your project or dissertation have a look at all the staff's profiles from the department where you are studying your degree programme.

Find out which member of staff has does research in an area that interests you. Book an appointment to speak with the person to discuss your ideas. Always go to the meetings with a list of questions and ideas on paper and this will show that you are organised. They will also recognise that you are serious about research and they will try to help you as much as they can, as it is also in their interest to see your research develop. Ask your tutors if they have a copy of titles of projects that have been studied before so that you can get an idea of topics that have been covered and choose something different.

When you have completed your dissertation or project report you will have written a small book. The amount of time and effort you put into that book will be rewarded with a good classification for your degree. Simple!

What I would like you to think about is writing around a subject or a piece of research that is going to make a difference to either a small concern eg. club, society, policy, school, group of people. Perhaps it could be a study around producing a poster or presentation so that you can go up on stage and present your findings to a group of people who will be interested in your research.

When you have completed your research, could the findings be published in a journal, could your research go towards a chapter in a book or could you continue your research into a bigger study for a doctorate or MPhil?

These are the considerations that students should be thinking about 'outside the box' when they want to write about a given subject.

Exercise 43: Presenting your research.

Write down a research idea, see what research is already out there. What theory is available to back up your arguments? Ask yourself would the research be costly to carry out eg. travel to carry out research, paper, printing, time off work etc.?

Speak with your tutors about this as they are the specialists in the field and they should know what is out there already.

Think about what you want to do with the research:

➢ This project only
➢ Present a paper
➢ Enter the research into a research journal
➢ Turn your research into a poster
➢ Contribute the research into a chapter in a book
➢ Extend your research project to achieve higher qualifications.

## Applying for postgraduate courses

Some students chose to do their PhD through peer reviewed published papers. This is very time consuming, but rewarding, as you are constantly working on different aspects within your field. There are numerous research opportunities that you can become involved in, through different organisations. The best website to find out about these is www.jobs.ac.uk. The pay for these research posts can be low but again it will give you the opportunity to be part of an organisation making a difference and showing the company or institution your skills. Through research you can then achieve some publications and heighten your personal profile. The majority of students decide to work with a supervisor to publish a thesis.

Universities are encouraging students to pursue master's study as they actively increase the research profile of the university.

A research excellence framework is now in place for universities to work towards, so the more research output eg. journal articles, peer reviewed research, research projects, books and contributions to chapters in books, then the higher the points that are awarded for the research excellence framework.

Sometimes students pursue a master's degree in a completely different subject to their undergraduate degree. If you are considering this, make sure you talk to students who have already done the course to find out what it involves.

An MA or MSc will have a large taught component and are similar to your final year of your degree but in much more depth.

Once a master's degree has been completed it is seen as a progression to carry in the same subject to an MPhil or PhD study. An MPhil is piece of research where you might typically write about 20,000 – 40,000 word dissertation as part of your final assessment.

A PhD thesis could be around 80,000 words but they can be much longer. With a PhD you should be seen to be making a difference to the field that you are studying in. You need to choose a research topic that you are passionate about as you are going to be spending a long time working on it. To pass you have to have "added to the body of man's knowledge." In other words you'll have discovered something no one knew before.

Just as the job market is competitive so is the application process for postgraduate study. You need to decide early which course suits your needs and find out about the timing of the process. Your careers office should be able to help you but also at this point, particularly for PhD study, it is time to talk to individual lecturers about the opportunities that might exist. Many lecturers have funding for students for particular projects from the relevant research council (www.rcuk.ac.uk).

### Case study: Postgraduate study?

Warren was really unsure what he wanted to do whilst in the final year of his degree programme and needed reassurance from his tutor that he was on line to receive a good classification for his degree. He needed to discuss what options were open to him to either complete a master's degree or to carry on working at his part time job in retail with a hope of gaining a graduate position within the company. The tutor discussed with Warren if he was prepared to move away from the area. He said that he wanted to stay local, to keep his part time job, look after his mum and family and also to travel to do the master's if this was going to be the option. The tutor discussed with Warren what his ultimate career goal was. He said that he wanted a job that included writing, sociology, not necessarily as part of a team and maybe freelance. Lots of options were discussed and at the end of the meeting Warren was encouraged to do some research into Master's degrees at local universities and to make contact with his employer to see what he could be earning if he were to take a graduate position. Another option for Warren was to carry on working part time to fund his master's programme, which in the end would lead to his dream job.

Exercise 44: Planning your postgraduate studies

Do you want to stay at your undergraduate University to pursue your master's, MPhil or PhD study?

Do you have a person in mind to be your research supervisor?

Would you want to complete you postgraduate study on a full or part time basis?

If on a part time basis, does the study time fit around your work time?

If full time, have you asked the department where you are going to undertake your postgraduate study whether there is some funding available to support your research, maybe as an associate tutor or research assistant?

Have you asked appropriate organisations if they are interested in your research ideas, as they may also have some funding available to support you?

Have you any ideas around the research questions you may want to cover in your research?

Will your research project be quantitative, qualitative or a mixture of the two and how will you present all your data?

Will your research be one big study or a series of papers?

**Case study: Returning to study**

Liam completed a degree programme at university three years ago. He was quite heavily involved in the professional world of sport and because of this his commitment to his degree programme fell by the wayside and his studies deteriorated. Liam had to re-do the second year of his degree programme again and graduated with a 2:2.

He was refused a place on a PGCE programme due to lack of experience and the fact that there were extremly limited places. Liam did not let this deter him and carried on playing professional rugby for a local team. He also became a teaching assistant in a local school as well as gaining coaching badges and other awards and travelling extensively with his team. Three years later Liam has been accepted onto a postgraduate programme and is working towards becoming a teacher in a secondary school.

## Presenting your Viva

A viva is an oral presentation of your work. Many courses now have either work placements or projects that have a mark for the presentation at the end. Many research degrees are also examined by a viva. At a viva you are not only expected to give a talk but you are also expected to spend a potion of the time answering in-depth questions about your work. You may be asked by any of your examiners to provide your raw data as well as your written summary. This means you should take with you any analysis that you have used to collect your research eg. questionnaires, task sheets, result sheets, consent forms, health declarations and risk assessments.

Make your presentation as dynamic and visual as you can as you can to showcase your work (have a look at the section on presentation skills). Check how long you'll have and make sure you leave time for questions.

### Make sure your presentation includes:

- ✓ Title of your research
- ✓ Aim of your research
- ✓ Methodology (the methods you are used to carry out your data analysis)
- ✓ Results you achieved
- ✓ Any conclusions
- ✓ Changes you'd make if you had the chance to do it again

### Work Placement viva:

- ✓ Title of the workplace
- ✓ Aim of the work placement
- ✓ What you did whilst there
- ✓ Comments from your supervisor
- ✓ What you learned from the placement.

> Exercise 45: Presenting your viva
>
> Include a Powerpoint presentation in your portfolio for your project or work placement.

## Preparing to Leave University

At the beginning of your final year of study you should be starting to analyse your goals in order to make plans for when you leave with your degree. The first thing to think about is updating your curriculum vitae to ensure that all the details are current and relevant and that your referees will still give you an outstanding reference (seek permission first before you put their names in your CV).

You should contact the careers department within the university. The careers department should have a directory of all the bigger companies that are offering graduate positions. The closing dates for these applications are often at the end of the calendar year, so you have three months once you return to University, in your final year, to apply and send off your applications.

Always get your application checked first either by your personal tutor, academic support tutor or a careers adviser.

There are hundreds of websites you can search through. You may wish to participate in some job shadowing. This will involve writing a letter to an employer and asking if you can work shadow them for a day or a week free of charge to enable you to get an insight into their role.

### Case study: Improving an application

Louise thought she'd finished her application for a job as a graduate trainee with a big firm. She took it along to the careers advisor. She had listed a whole range of skills such as good team building skills, time management, listening skills etc. but she hadn't provided any specific examples.

The careers advisor got her to think about when she'd used the skills and to provide details. Here is what she came up with for team building.

"I had a part time job as a waitress with a small, family run catering company. Initially when we went to some of the events, like weddings, it seemed a bit chaotic. After I'd helped out a few times I saw that the problem was that everyone was getting in each other's way and some jobs weren't getting done, people were getting upset. I suggested to the manager that it would make sense if everyone had specific roles and were given responsibility for that area. She agreed with me and at the next event she gave everyone instructions on what was their responsibility. After that it seemed to run much more smoothly."

141

## Applying for Employment

The letter of application is the most important document you will produce as it will go to the human resource department in a company who will then make a decision as to whether your application will go forward for interview or selection. You must be able to describe clear examples of how you are suitable for the post by selling your skills and providing excellent examples of how you have applied those skills to your experiences.

Possible skills to demonstrate are:

- ✓ Organisational skills
- ✓ Time management skills
- ✓ Communication skills
- ✓ Motivational skills
- ✓ Presentation skills
- ✓ Problem solving skills
- ✓ IT skills
- ✓ Analytical skills
- ✓ Team working skills

Unfortunately today you have to be prepared to go that extra mile to achieve your goal. This may involve working voluntarily for a company, work shadowing for a short time or being prepared to start at the bottom of the company knowing you are more than qualified for the position that is on offer.

You need to start applying for graduate positions stating on your CV that you are attending university, that your degree course is ongoing and you are online to graduate with an estimated degree classification (be honest with this you may get asked at interview to provide your current marks).

You need to ask your careers department for specialist websites for jobs and careers in your degree areas or look back at chapter 4 of this book and look at some of the websites provided.

Exercise 46: Applying for Employment

Carry out a job search for three relevant jobs in your area. Looking at the job descriptions, identify the skills they are looking for. Download the jobs and highlight the skills.

Write about how you would use each of the skills below and give examples of experience where you have had to apply those relevant skills (see previously):

## Letter of Application

This is the way that you sell yourself to at least get an interview. Your letter should be in a business format. Following are samples of a letter of application for employment and a letter to apply for a placement opportunity.

It is really important that you present your skills and say what you can offer the company that you are applying for.

Address your letter to the person who is going to employ you. If you do use the person's name then finish your letter off with Yours sincerely. If you don't know the name of the person you are writing to then address as Dear Sir/Madam, then at the end of your letter end it with Yours faithfully.

Make sure the font easy to read such as 12 point Arial or Calibri.

Be really positive throughout your letter. Avoid making negative comments which will go against your application eg. 'as you can see my experience is limited'.

Make sure you address the person specification and job description as this a way of keeping your statements relevant and to the point.

**Please remember to sign your letter.**

**Here is an example of a letter of application for a post:**

44 Neston Drive
Southport
PR8 322
Tel 01744 532432
20th February 20XX

Mr C. Marquard
Director of Financial Services
Marquard and Fynch Ltd
Temple Square
Liverpool
L1 2ZZ

Dear Mr Marquard,

I am writing to apply for the post of ................. advertised in the Liverpool echo dated .............

As you will see from the enclosed CV, I have specialised in management and e-business and can offer valuable skills and knowledge that will contribute to your stated aim of being at the forefront of the financial services industry.

I have also carried out projects in enterprise development and financial management marketing. These have developed my commercial awareness and knowledge of best practice in today's successful companies.

My enthusiasm, commitment and high level of self-motivation allow me to contribute to situations requiring initiative and flair and I can demonstrate considerable ability as a team player with leadership qualities.

I am confident that the opportunities provided by Marquard and Fynch as a key player in the financial services industry are ideally suited to my knowledge, ability and career direction.

I look forward to having the opportunity to provide further evidence of my suitability for the post.

Yours sincerely,

Paul Stevens.

# LETTER OF APPLICATION

**Here is an example of a letter asking for a work shadowing or placement opportunity.**

74 Holy Bank Road
Ashton in Makerfield
Lancashire
L39 42QL

Mrs J Smith                                                        17th March 20XX
Manager – Play scheme UK
Sport within a community project
St Aldreds Catholic College, Winchester
WN1 4BX

Dear Mrs Smith,

I am currently in my second year at University, studying for a BA (Hons) degree in Media and Journalism and I am writing to ask whether you will have any summer jobs available working at the Children's Play scheme. I enclose my CV for your perusal.

Over the past few years I have gained a great deal of experience in working with young people. I work voluntarily as a swimming instructor at my local swimming club. As part of my degree course, I have also undertaken a placement in a primary school with children in Year 6. I have also gained experienced working in the USA as a Camp Counsellor last summer, where I was responsible for a group of young people of 11/12 years of age. I have also of organised activities in sport, drama and other pursuits as part of the course. This also allowed me to travel extensively all over the U.S. getting involved with lots of other sports and people from a variety of cultural backgrounds.

I am reliable and trustworthy as my final report, a copy of which is available on request, from my camp supervisors demonstrates. Enclosed also are my other employer references.

I am aware that the Children's Play scheme has been running very successfully for a number of years in the Community. Some of the children I spoke to on placement at school had used the scheme and enjoyed it immensely. I would like very much to use my skills and experience to help maintain its excellent reputation.

I am available for interview at your convenience. If you require any further details please do not hesitate to contact me.

Yours sincerely,

Emma Partington

Exercise 47: Write a letter of application for a post or a work placement that is advertised at the moment.
Add it to your portfolio.

**Case study: How not to prepare for an interview**

Peter was on the senior management team and was asked to be on an interview panel for a new graduate job. One interviewee had travelled over 150 miles for the interview.

Each member of the interview panel asked different questions. Peter asked his first question, "What do you know about our company?" The interviewee had absolutely no clue. He obviously hadn't even visited the company website. Immediately he'd failed to get the job, the rest of the interview was a waste of time. Peter said "All he needed to have done was spend an hour before he came finding out some simple things about our company. It just showed a complete lack of initiative. How could he justify wanting to work for us when he had no clue about what we do?"

## Job Applications

More and more companies nowadays are asking applicants to apply online for job vacancy posts. If this is the case then it is really important for you to make sure that your typing skills are adequate to allow you to complete the application, save a copy so that you can refer to it, if you get invited for interview.

If you are required to send a typed application form by post then again it is important that you complete all the relevant areas that the company is asking for information. So many people leave boxes blank when they just need to have a n/a added (short for not applicable), so that the company knows that you have not forgotten to complete the relevant questions. Sometimes there is insufficient space for all your qualifications or work experience or continued professional development. If this is the case then in the box on the application form simply add 'see enclosed sheet'. Then you can list all your additional information on separate sheets and include it in your application.

Make sure that when you are providing references that you include the names, addresses, email addresses and telephone numbers. This is the information a prospective employer will need should they decide to give you an interview. Do not put on your application 'references on request'. Make sure you give as much information as possible. You will be asked on the application form to provide examples of how you are suitable for the post. You need to give specific examples not broad statements such as "I've got great communication skills." This way you can also include your curriculum vitae.

When a job application arrives in a Human Resource department there may be thousands of other applications for the same job, it is up to you to make your application stand out from all the rest. Cream, good quality paper is an excellent way to make your letter of application and curriculum vitae stand out, as all the rest of the applications will be on white paper and the future employer will see that you have gone to an extra effort. Don't leave it until the last posting day to get in your application to the company either, the earlier the better.

You can always book an appointment with a careers advisor at your university who will be really happy to look over covering letters, layout of your curriculum vitae and application forms. Some universities offer this service for one year after leaving university.

148

# Interviews

As part of your final year programme it has been successfully proven that undergraduates benefit from going through a mock interview process.

This can be set up between members of academic staff and or employers who sit on the panel asking questions to the candidate as if in a real interview session. (See interview questions). If your department doesn't have mock interviews ask the careers department if they can help you.

A real job is advertised either on the notice board, through the VLE (virtual learning environment) or email. The students are then encouraged to apply for the post, submitting a letter of application, application form and CV. This way the interviewers get to write all over the application and can give feedback on whether the candidate would be successful or not at interview. This is a really important process as most graduates don't get past the application stage of the interview process. Interviews can also be set up for placement opportunities or industrial experience. This way the undergraduate gets through the nervousness before going into the world of work.

It is important that graduates understand that if they are asked to go for an interview that personal presentation plays a really large part and attitude is key!

Here is a list of things to consider:

**Guys:**

✓ Jewellery must be minimal
✓ Fasten the top button under your tie
✓ Wear dark socks under your suit
✓ Preferably have your jacket matching your trousers
✓ Wear dark shoes so that they are a darker colour than your trousers
✓ Make sure your hair is neat
✓ Wear aftershave, but not too much
✓ Make sure your nails are clean
✓ Wear deodorant/antiperspirant

**Girls:**

- ✓ Make sure you wear tights or trouser socks
- ✓ Wear darker shoes than the colour of your hemline
- ✓ Wear underwear that does not show through your clothing
- ✓ Make sure skirts/ dresses are knee length
- ✓ Light make-up is desirable as this will make you look more professional
- ✓ Neat business type handbag to match the colour of your shoes
- ✓ Navy blue/black are the most preferred colours to wear for interviews
- ✓ Minimal perfume as too much can be too overpowering

**Everyone:**

- ✓ Research the company before your interview (see exercise 37) Always remember check your body language and posture
- ✓ Sit comfortably, hands together, feet slightly apart, open gestures
- ✓ Maintain eye contact with whoever is speaking to you at the time
- ✓ Smile politely, use manners but not overly politely
- ✓ At the end of the interview ask one or two questions, no more
- ✓ Thank the interviewers for their time

**Case study: Answering questions**

Stacey was not confident about her ability to answer questions in interviews. She had some confidence building sessions with her tutor on interview skills. She wrote down the answers to possible questions (see following) that may be asked at interview. Her tutor then asked her the questions and encouraged Stacey to look up at the tutor's face when answering the questions, something Stacey found extremely uncomfortable. Three sessions later and the process became much easier and the result is that she was accepted onto a higher degree to study to become a primary school teacher, her lifetime ambition.

Exercise 48: Have a think about some of these typical interview questions.

Tell me about yourself.

....................................................................................

....................................................................................

Why did you apply for the job?

....................................................................................

....................................................................................

What do you know about this company? (see exercise 37)

....................................................................................

....................................................................................

Tell me what you do in your spare time.

....................................................................................

....................................................................................

What are your main strengths and weaknesses?

....................................................................................

....................................................................................

Why should we employ you?

....................................................................................

....................................................................................

What have you learned from your past work experiences?

....................................................................................

....................................................................................

When did you last work under pressure or deal with conflict and how did you cope with the situation?

....................................................................................

....................................................................................

151

What is the biggest problem or dilemma you have ever faced?

What other career opportunities are you looking at?

Where would you like to be in five or ten years time?

What would you do in ........ situation?

So sell me this product.

What salary do you expect?

How competent are you at......?

Do you have any questions?

## Summary

As you can see many of these interview questions are very similar to the reflective questions we've used in the exercises over the course.

You need to consider how you are going to track your professional development over your career. It is highly likely that you will be changing jobs, and possibly careers, five to ten times in your working life. You need to consider having an on-going portfolio to record your thoughts and store details of any training courses you attend.

Each year look at your list of dreams and I'm sure you'll be ticking some of them off and perhaps adding a few. Set aside time to undertake goal planning over different time scales and plan to do one new development activity per month, be it a training session, new challenge or reading a book.

# Final Thoughts

I hope you have found this book useful in helping you to build your own personal development planning portfolio. This should have helped you to gain the skills which will help you through your degree or college programmes in preparation for industry.

Remember there are lots of other free resources on the website www.uolearn.com, including many of the forms.

I really hope that this book has given you real food for thought and that you will realise that anything in life is achievable. It is all about taking small steps to get there.

Good luck and all the best in your chosen careers.

Love and light,

Angela

**Notes:**

**Notes:**

# Bibliography

Arnold,R., (1993). Time Management. Leamington Spa: Scholastic.

Belbin Team Roles, (2007). http://www.belbin.com/ [accessed 5th November 2010].

Burgess Report, (2007). Beyond the honours degree classification Publications. The Burgess Group final report. http//www.universities.ac.uk/Publications.16/10/2007. [accessed 13th August 2010].

Burns,T. Sinfield,S., (2009). Essential study skills. The Complete Guide to Success at University. London: Sage Publications Ltd.

Caroseli,M., (2000). Leadership skills for managers (electronic resource. New York: McGraw Hill.

Centre for Recording Achievement, http://www.centre for recordingachievement.org [accessed 6th November 2010].

Clark,A., (2004). e-Learning Skills. Hampshire: Palgrave Macmillan.

Cottrell,S., (2003). The Study Skills Handbook. Second edition. Hampshire: Palgrave Macmillan.

Cottrell,S., (2003). Skills for success. The Personal Development Handbook. Hampshire: Palgrave Macmillan.

Cottrell,S., (2001). Teaching Study Skills and Supporting Learning. Hampshire: Palgrave Macmillan.

Crisfield,P., (1994). Time management: Balance sport, work and home more effectively. English Sports Council: National Coaching Foundation.

Dearing report., (1997). NCIHE (National Committee of Inquiry into Higher Education) Higher Education in the Learning Society, (the Dearing Report) London: HMSO.

Fanthorne,C., (2004). Work placements- A survival guide for students. New York: Palgrave Macmillan.

Forster,M., (2000). Get Everything Done and Still have Time to Play. London, Hodder and Stoughton

Foskett,N. and Foskett,R., (2006). Postgraduate Study in the UK. The International students Guide. London: Sage Publications.

Gosling,D., (1994). Personal Development Planning. London: Seda Papers.

Greenhall,M., (2011). Speed Reading Skills Training Course. Lancashire: Universe of Learning

Greetham,B., (2001). How to Write Better Essays. Hampshire: Palgrave Macmillan.

Harris,I. Caviglioli,O., (2003). Think it-map it! Great Britain: MPG Books.

Harvey, L., (2004). Analytic Quality Glossary, Quality Research International. http://www.qualityresearchinternational.com/ glossary/

Knight,T.and Yorke,M., (2003). England: Open University Press.

Kolb,D., (1984). Experiential Learning, Eaglewood Cliffs, New Jersey, Prentice Hall.

Littleford,D. Halstead,J. Mulraine,C., (2004). Career Skills Opening Doors into the Job Market. Hampshire: Palgrave Macmillan.

Maddock,R.C., (1998). Motivation, Emotions and Leadership: The silent side of management. WesportConn; London Quorum.

McWhorter,K.T., (2000). Study and Critical thinking skills in college. USA: Quebec Printing.

Moon,J., (1999). Learning journals. A handbook for academics, students and professional development, London. Kogan Page.

Northedge,A., (2007). The good Study Guide. Milton Keynes: Open University.

Peck,J. Coyle,M., (1999). The student's guide to writing, Grammar punctuation and spelling. Hampshire: Palgrave Macmillan.

Staffordshire University, (2010). Writing a Literature Review. http://www.staff.ac.uk/uniservices/studyskills/factfiles/literature_ review.pdf/ [accessed June 2010].

QAAHE. (1999). QAA policy on programme specification, www.qaa. ac.uk/crntwork/spec.[accessed 12th November 2010].

QAAHE, (2001). Guidelines for H.E Progress Files. Gloucester, Quality Assurance agency for Higher Education.

Ros,J., (2002). Time Management. Oxford:Capstone Publishing.

Wilson,G., (2000). Problem Solving. London: Kogan Page.

# Universe of Learning Books

"The purpose of learning is growth, and our minds, unlike our bodies, can continue growing as we continue to live." Mortimer Adler

# About the publishers

Universe of Learning Limited is a small publisher based in the UK with production in England and America. Our authors are all experienced trainers or teachers who have taught their skills for many years. We are actively seeking qualified authors and if you visit the authors section on www.uolearn.com you can find out how to apply.

If you are interested in any of our current authors (including Angela Hepworth) coming to speak at your event please do visit their own websites (to contact Angela please email angela@ uolearn.com) or email them through the author section of the uolearn site.

If you would like to purchase larger numbers of books then please do contact us (sales@uolearn.com). We give discounts from 5 books upwards.  For larger volumes we can also quote for changes to the cover to accommodate your company logo and to the interior to brand it for your company.

All our books are written by teachers, trainers or people well experienced in their roles and our goal is to help people develop their skills with a well structured range of exercises.

If you have any feedback about this book or other topics that you'd like to see us cover please do contact us at support@uolearn.com.

To buy the printed books please order from your favourite bookshop, including Amazon, Waterstones, Blackwells and Barnes and Noble. For ebooks please visit www.uolearn.com.

Keep Learning!

# Speed Writing

## Speedwriting for faster note taking and dictation

ISBN 978-1-84937-011-0, from www.uolearn.com

Easy exercises to learn faster writing in just 6 hours.

✓ "The principles are very easy to follow, and I am already using it to take notes."
✓ "I will use this system all the time."
✓ "Your system is so easy to learn and use."

# Report Writing

## An easy to follow format for writing reports

ISBN 978-1-84937-036-3, from www.uolearn.com

This book makes report writing a step by step process for you to follow every time you have a report to write.

✓ How to set objectives using 8 simple questions
✓ Easy to follow flow chart
✓ How to write an executive summary
✓ How to layout and structure the report
✓ Help people remember what they read

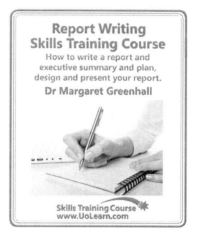

# Speed Reading Skills Training Course

## How to read a book, report or short document on paper or online three times as fast with comprehension for study skills and business

ISBN: 978-1-84937-021-9, Order at www.uolearn.com

Would you like to learn simple techniques to help you read 3 times as fast?

This book has a series of easy to follow guided exercises that help you change your reading habits to both read faster and to evaluate which parts to read and in what order.

# Study Skills Training Course

**How to pass your exam, test or coursework easily**

Improve your learning skills to pass exams and assessments, take notes, memorize facts and speed read, for studying at school and college

ISBN: 978-1-84937-020-2, Order at www.uolearn.com

Dr Greenhall's techniques helped her to get a first class honours degree in physics and chemistry, a doctorate in science and an MA in education, easily and with little effort. Guided exercises will help you to learn the secrets of these successes.

# How to Start a Business as a Private Tutor

ISBN 978-1-84937-029-5, from www.uolearn.com

This book, by a Lancashire based author, shows you how to set up your own business as a tutor.

- ✓ Packed with tips and stories
- ✓ How to get started - what to do and buy
- ✓ How to attract clients and advertise
- ✓ Free printable forms, ready to use
- ✓ Advice on preparing students for exams

# Successful Minute Taking Meeting the Challenge

**How to prepare, write and organise agendas and minutes of meetings**

ISBN 978-1-84937-040-0, from www.uolearn.com

- ✓ Becoming more confident in your role
- ✓ A checklist of what to do
- ✓ Help with layout and writing skills
- ✓ Learn what to include in minutes
- ✓ How to work well with your chairperson

Learn to be an excellent meeting secretary.

# Coaching Skills Training Course

## Business and life coaching techniques for

ISBN: 978-1-84937-019-6, from www.uolearn.com
- ✓ An easy to follow 5 step model
- ✓ Learn to both self-coach and coach others
- ✓ Over 25 ready to use ideas
- ✓ Goal setting tools to help achieve ambitions

A toolbox of ideas to help you become a great coach

# Stress Management

## Exercises and techniques to manage stress and anxiety

ISBN: 978-1-84937-002-8, from www.uolearn.com
- ✓ Understand what stress is
- ✓ Become proactive in managing your stress
- ✓ Learn how to change your response to stress
- ✓ How to become more positive about your life
- ✓ An easy 4 step model to lasting change

# Practical and Effective Performance Management

ISBN: 978-1-84937-037-0, from www.uolearn.com
- ✓ Five key ideas to understanding performance
- ✓ A clear four step model
- ✓ Key what works research that is practical
- ✓ A large, wide ranging choice of tools
- ✓ Practical exercises and action planning for managers.
  A toolbox of ideas to help you become a better leader.

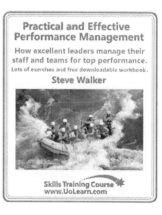

# Developing Your Influencing Skills

ISBN: 978-1-84937-004-2, from www.uolearn.com
- ✓ Decide what your influencing goals are
- ✓ Find ways to increase your credibility rating
- ✓ Develop stronger and more trusting relationships
- ✓ Inspire others to follow your lead
- ✓ Become a more influential communicator

Packed with case studies, exercises and practical tips to become more influential.

"Don't wait until everything is just right.
It will never be perfect. There will always be challenges,
obstacles and less than perfect conditions.
So what. Get started now.
With each step you take, you will grow stronger and
stronger, more and more skilled, more and more
self-confident and more and more successful."
Mark Victor Hansen

Lightning Source UK Ltd.
Milton Keynes UK
UKOW012349020212

186507UK00004B/88/P